P ... n™:

'*ToddlerCalm*™ is a must-read for all parents and professionals working with toddlers. The book is packed with tips, ideas and positive stories from other parents. It reached deep into the heart and soul of understanding what makes little people tick. This book is essential reading for any parent feeling "out on a limb"'
Marneta Viegas, founder of Relax Kids

'A kind, well-written description of what it means to be a toddler and how parents can guide and support toddlers as they begin that long journey to being a strong, healthy child and then adult. With the tools and stories presented here, parents will be able to see their toddlers in a new light and understand the importance of their role in helping them to learn and grow'
Wendy Middlemiss, Associate Professor of Educational Psychology, University of North Texas

'Everything you say in the book resonates with the way we hope will parent.'

Dame Sarah Storey

'I like the fact that *ToddlerCalm*™ is written in a non-judgemental way. It offers support and guidance to parents and I find myself dipping in and out of it for advice and reassurance ... I dreaded "circle time" at the various parent/toddler groups I went to. If I had read this book first I wouldn't have felt the need to persevere and my toddler and I would have happily pottered at home instead of feeling we always had to be so busy!'
Nell McAndrew, model and marathon runner

'*ToddlerCalm*™ is a fantastic blend of science and compassion which enables you to parent from your heart and gives an insight into the frustrations our little people feel whilst giving us some fabulous tools to help them through their struggles'
Caroline Osborne, participant in a ToddlerCalm™
parenting class

'*ToddlerCalm*™ gave me confidence to trust my instincts and calmly work through my toddler's big emotions with her – instead of throwing tantrums myself!'
Adele Jarrett-Kerr, participant in a ToddlerCalm™
parenting class

ToddlerCalm

A guide for
calmer toddlers
&
happier parents

Sarah Ockwell-Smith

Foreword by **Dr Oliver James**

piatkus

PIATKUS

First published in Great Britain in 2013 by Piatkus
Reprinted 2013 (twice), 2014 (twice)

A CIP catalogue record for this book
is available from the British Library.

ISBN 978-0-349-40105-8

Illustrations by Rodney Paull
Typeset in Stone Serif by M Rules
Printed and bound in Great Britain by
Clays Ltd, St Ives plc

Papers used by Piatkus are from well-managed forests
and other responsible sources.

MIX
Paper from
responsible sources
FSC® C104740

Piatkus
An imprint of
Little, Brown Book Group
100 Victoria Embankment
London EC4Y 0DY

An Hachette UK Company
www.hachette.co.uk

www.piatkus.co.uk

For Sebastian, Flynn, Rafferty and Violet
I love you most.

About the author

Sarah Ockwell-Smith is a well-known UK-based parenting expert. She is famed for her gentle, science-rich, yet easy-to-read books and blog, which are read and recommended by thousands of parents and professionals worldwide.

Born in Bedfordshire, England in 1976, Sarah Ockwell-Smith is the mother of four school-aged children, three boys and one girl. Sarah lives with her husband, children, three cats and numerous chickens in a 400-year-old cottage in rural Essex.

Sarah initially studied psychology at university, after which she embarked on a five-year career in pharmaceutical research and development until she became pregnant with her first child in 2001. After the birth of her firstborn Sarah retrained as a homeopath, HypnoBirthing teacher and doula providing for a rather eclectic mix of scientific and holistic viewpoints. Since then Sarah has worked with over a thousand parents, helping them to prepare for and settle into life as a new family through her antenatal classes, birth and postnatal doula support, homeopathic consultations and workshops and BabyCalm™ groups. BabyCalm™ started life in Sarah's living room in 2007 as a response to requests from the parents she had worked with for more support after the birth of their babies and, due to huge public demand, five years later in 2012 Sarah launched ToddlerCalm™, focusing on life with children aged one to four.

Sarah is concerned by the numbers of popular 'parenting experts' giving strong opinions with little or no scientific evidence (or even parenting experience of their own!) to back up their claims. When writing her books Sarah wanted to help parents not only to calm and understand their children, but also to help them to trust their instincts and make their own parenting decisions, confidently, without relying on somebody else's routines or manuals. Sarah herself is uncomfortable with being referred to as a 'parenting expert' for she feels the only people qualified enough to bear this title are the parents themselves. Indeed, her biggest fear is people recognising her when she is out in public with her unruly brood!

Contents

Acknowledgements

would like to thank my husband, Ian, and my children, Seb, Flynn, Raff and Violet, for putting up with my snappy moods and lack of attention while I wrote my second book in as many years. I am so very proud of the people that you are all becoming, despite my muddled efforts at parenting you. In the spirit of modelling self-praise I would like to add that, yes, mummy is proud of herself too. I feel like I have accomplished so much in the last two years but I couldn't have done any of it without your help; nothing makes me more proud though than when you tell me how proud you are of me!

Huge thanks are due to clinical child psychologist Dr Victoria Montgomery, for her knowledge, insight and support in helping me to develop the ToddlerCalm™ programme and in continuing to help me to constantly improve it. If you happen to live near Cambridge, England you should definitely try to get along to one of Vic's ToddlerCalm™ courses or workshops. I guarantee that you will learn an awful lot from her.

A big thank you must go to those parents who have offered their stories, warts and all, for publication in this book. I do think that their stories make this book come alive and it wouldn't be the same without them.

Lastly, a big thanks to all of the ToddlerCalm™ team, from those working behind the scenes to make it all happen to those 'on the front line' working with parents. Bring on the revolution!

Foreword

On average, an eighteen-month old will try and take a toy from another eight times an hour. At two and a half, they are still doing that four times an hour.

In this book, Sarah Ockwell-Smith provides the best account I have read of why they do this and the different ways to respond. Parents of all kinds would do well to 'read, learn and inwardly digest', as my teachers used to say to me.

Toddlers have not yet developed a 'pause' button for regulating their emotions and actions. Still lacking sophisticated language, they naturally will use action to assert themselves. Whilst sometimes they can use words to express their wishes, when frustrated, they have yet to develop the parts of the brain which enable them to delay gratification, to put off getting what they want, which at their age, they feel should happen by magic. It is out of their relationship with carers, especially mothers, that the pause button part of the brain evolves.

For nearly two decades parents have been inundated with books and television programmes advocating strict imposition of rules for under threes. In many cases, this simply does not work.

Worse still, in some cases, it does!

The result is a seemingly obedient, even friendly child but not very deep beneath the surface is a surly, growling, miserable beast. Either he becomes a sneaky and unpleasant child, as soon as the adults' backs are turned, a troublemaker for peers or a secret rule-breaker, who becomes the aggressive or hyperactive one in the primary school class. Or else, he becomes a withdrawn, passive creature, scared of life, who becomes the depressed, sad primary school child. If you want either of those, fine, implement a regime of naughty steps and early potty training. But if you want a cheerful, playful, happy child, read this book for the alternative.

What toddlers need is to be allowed to live in la-la land, to live in a world of playful wonder, ideally accompanied by a sympathetic and responsive adult. Like Peter Pan, all they want to do is play. If they are not allowed to do that, they become the Pan of fiction, a boy who cannot grow up.

Of course, along the way, from time to time, they also need to be made aware of external realities. The older they get, the greater the necessity to make them aware that biting other children causes pain and that slinging food on the floor does not make mummy happy. But bringing them into land in the adult world needs to be done gradually and with understanding of their limitations. Failure to do so makes it far more likely they will crash and burn, in the long term. Paradoxically, independence only is possible if dependence and self-preoccupation have been permitted.

This book is not an instruction manual. There are no strict rules for helping your toddler gradually get his head around the hard fact that the world often does not magically accord with his wishes, any more than being 'strict' with the child will result in a creative and self-motivated adult. There has been far too much strictness on the part of experts towards parents, just as there has been too much strict care of toddlers.

I welcome this book as a sensitive antidote to the alternatives. It is not advocating permissive or authoritarian care, it is a paean to the glorious fun and joy which can result from understanding your toddler, seeing it from their point of view, and then gently nudging them towards maturity.

Dr Oliver James

Introduction

Terrible twos, threenagers, tantrums, biting, hitting, whining, picky eating, toilet training troubles, sleep problems, the list goes on. There's no doubt about it: parenting a toddler is hard. Really hard. To add to this it is often the time that many decide to add a new baby to their family, which brings a whole new set of different demands and often doubles the exhaustion that parents face.

You've survived the first year of parenthood. The sleepless nights and cluster feeding demands of a newborn, then the broken nights and soothing the cries of a teething baby in pain. You've tackled weaning, baby proofed your home when your little one became mobile and some of you have successfully negotiated your return to work. Only now, just as your confidence had reached a new parental high and you had some idea of what you were doing, you've reached the scary domain of toddlerdom and in many ways feel like you're right back at the beginning again. Gone is your warm, snuggly, immobile baby bundle and in its place is a wilful ball of curious energy, fighting for control and independence and leaving a trail of devastation behind them. A toddler who causes you much joy on the good days, but also heartache, frustration and embarrassment, particularly when they tantrum in public, on a shopping trip, at a family party, in front of your friend and her perfect, non-tantruming child and worst of all in the presence of your mother-in-law, whose own children 'never acted like that'.

I would be the first person to admit how hard I found the toddler years with my own four children. I think many people expect parenting authors to have had perfect children and know all of the answers. I didn't. I frequently felt like tearing my hair out and screaming at the top of my lungs. In fact one day, one really bad day, when my firstborn was around eighteen months old, I remember having a conversation with a friend and wistfully thinking that perhaps it might be nice to commit a petty crime and be sent to prison for a little while, in order to have a short spell away from my toddler, nobody screaming 'mummeeee' constantly, a trip to the toilet in peace, a bed to myself, space to think and blissful quiet. I don't want that to sound like I am advocating crime; of course I don't, I'm merely highlighting quite how exhausted and desperate I felt with the overwhelming demands of parenting a toddler. I don't think there is a parent out there who hasn't despaired of their toddler at times and reached the end of their tether, or a parent who hasn't wanted not to be near their own child or hasn't reminisced about the quiet and calm days, when they were fully in control, pre-children. Even the perfect parents, they have bad days too, I promise you, and they're not really perfect.

I searched high and low to find 'the answer'. I read books with enticing titles which promised to solve all of my problems, only they didn't; they just made me feel even more confused and inadequate as a parent. I bought reward charts, hundreds of stickers, an alarm clock with a bunny rabbit face, which was meant to solve our sleeping dilemmas, five different potties and goodness knows how many sweets to use as rewards. I sought help from medical sources, from friends and from magazines and I religiously watched any toddler behaviour related programmes on television, each one of them advising something different and many driving me to tears for the way the toddlers were being treated. After a shaky start I had eventually found the baby years quite instinctive, but my instinct had left the building by the time I had a two-year-old.

I'll openly admit I made mistakes with my first child, and in fact with all of my children, as we all do. I did things with them and to them that make me cringe now I know better. I am only too grateful that they have turned out as fantastically as they have despite their mother inflicting all sorts of psychological trauma on them. The thing is we all make mistakes, no parent is perfect, parenting is a journey and we all have to start somewhere. That's where ToddlerCalm™ comes in. After the launch of BabyCalm™ workshops and classes I was inundated with requests from parents to create a course to help them with their toddlers, so ToddlerCalm™ was born entirely out of public demand and now we have teachers all over the world running courses and workshops that help parents to understand their toddlers and formulate a plan of action to cope with all sorts of frustrating behaviour from sleepless nights to picky eating, tantrums to biting. Naturally the calls for a ToddlerCalm™ book came very shortly after the launch of the classes and that is where this book comes in. I hope to share some of the things I have learnt with you on my own journey and a little of what we cover in our workshops, including my unique CRUCIAL toddler parenting strategy. CRUCIAL (Control, Rhythm, Understanding, Communication, Individual, Avoiding, Love) is an acronym I developed not only to help parents understand their toddler's needs and behaviour, but also to act as an empowering framework to help them to solve their own parenting dilemmas in their own way.

I strongly believe there is no one 'right way' to raise a toddler, in fact quite the reverse; parenting should be individual for each and every family. How one parent tackles a problem with their child will be, and should be, very different to how another might. We are all individuals and it concerns me that most parenting experts ignore this fact when they tell families what to do to tame their little horrors (their words, not mine). This is something I will strongly keep in mind throughout this book: the point of individuality and personal choice, hopefully helping you to make a plan of the best way forward for you and your individual child.

Have you ever noticed how many follow-up books most parenting authors write? You know the famous ones you see on television, the books that are in every shop on the high street. Why do you think this is? Surely if what they were saying was really helping parents there would be no need for the follow-up books? The problem here is by pitching themselves as 'the experts' with all of 'the answers' the parents are left feeling that they couldn't possibly be an expert in their own children. They remain forever in need of the next book and the next so that they can read the right way to handle new situations and developmental periods they are facing.

I do not want to be like all of the other parenting experts: I have accepted now that people will call me a 'parenting expert' although it is a term I will never be comfortable with. My aim for this book is to produce something that will empower you, a book that will contain everything you need in order to be a confident parent who can tackle any situation your toddler might throw at you (sometimes literally). I don't want to write a toddler sleep book, a toddler eating book, a toddler behaviour book, a toddler potty training book, a toddler and new sibling book, a toddler twins book and so on, although I admit the thought of stacking up the royalties is quite appealing. You see, if I did write an entire toddler related series I really wouldn't be empowering you. Quite simply I hope that this book will be the only one that you need to read, giving you all the tools to parent confidently throughout the first five years of your child's life and sometimes beyond. You already know more about your own toddler than I ever will; you are already an expert on your own toddler. I'm just here to fill in the gaps, as you might say. This beautiful quote by playwright George Bernard Shaw sums up my feelings about my role: 'I'm not a teacher: only a fellow-traveller of whom you asked the way. I pointed ahead – ahead of myself as well as you.'

Throughout the rest of this book I will help you to understand your toddler's behaviour. To start with we will take a whistle-stop tour of paediatric neuropsychology, in order to help you understand the way your toddler's brain works (it's quite different to yours). We will look at the work of some of the child psychology greats, past and present. We'll look at the biology of taste and sleep and consider what might really be normal for a toddler. We'll look at the most common forms of toddler behavioural control methods in use today, specifically naughty steps/corners, time out, reward charts and praise, and consider whether they are as great and useful as they first seem, and we'll consider some alternatives. We'll also discover quite how much you matter and how important it is for you to take care of yourself and sometimes put your own needs first and why your own moods affect your child's. Then we'll consider some specific situations commonly faced by parents of toddlers and apply our new knowledge and understanding to them. Hopefully by the end of the book you will have formed an action plan for your own parenting concerns. Throughout I hope to illustrate my points with plenty of real life examples and stories from myself and other parents, all of whom have faced struggles with their own toddlers, perhaps some similar to you.

With this new understanding hopefully I can help you to appreciate quite how wonderful and amazing your toddler really is. Parenting a toddler can be, and is, hard, but it can also be one of the most fun and rewarding experiences you will ever have.

That really is what this book is all about, helping you to enjoy nearly every moment with your toddler, because soon, very soon, your little toddler will be a big strapping child, no longer able to curl up on your lap, sit on your shoulders or fit in your arms when you tenderly carry them sleeping from the car. These years are magical, but they go so very quickly and all too often are lost in the trauma of public tantrums, the stress of night waking and the tears of wondering what you did wrong to create such a monster. My aim is to help you enjoy these precious years while they last and to help you build the foundations for a loving, empathic relationship with your toddler that will provide the ground works for the years to come. Yes, toddlers are hard work but they are also funny, inquisitive, entertaining, loving and great companions. We just need to be in a position to see that and hopefully with a little bit of my help you'll get there very soon!

Chapter 1

Who do I want my toddler to be?

If we are worried about the future, then we must look today at the upbringing of children.

Gordon B. Hinckley, religious leader and author

What are your hopes for your toddler's future? It goes without saying that we hope our children will grow up to be happy and healthy and preferably financially secure, but what are your aspirations for your toddler's personality? What qualities do you hope that he will possess when he is grown?

Before we move on I would like to ask you quickly to note down ten qualities you hope your child will possess when he is an adult. For instance, you might hope that he will be confident, independent, empathic and kind or perhaps you might like him to have a natural curiosity about the world, to question things and have good morals. There are no right or wrong answers here, but my hopes are that this short exercise will help you begin to formulate a plan to cope with your toddler's behaviour that we will add to with each new chapter of the book.

1. _____

2. _____

3. _____

4. _____

5. _____

6. _____

7. _____

8. _____

9. _____

10. _____

Short term versus long term parenting roles

Now take a look at your list. I imagine it is full of inspiring and positive words that might seem a long way off when you look at your stubborn, whining, non-sleeping toddler. But are these qualities really that far out of reach?

Isn't it ironic? When we parent a toddler we are always concerned about teaching them right from wrong, disciplining them so that they can learn how to live in a sociable world. We teach them to share and to say please and thank you; we do everything we can to keep them safe and goodness knows how hard that is when we have a toddler who tries to open bottles of bleach, would make a grab for the fire the second your head is turned and dashes for the stairs the minute somebody accidentally leaves the stairgate open. We are mindful that our toddlers should learn that it is not acceptable to tantrum in public in order to get their way, or shove another child at playgroup because they are playing with a toy they wanted. We want them to grow to be independent and encourage them to not be shy or rely on us too much; we want them to be healthy, so we spend hours tempting them to eat, making train and aeroplane noises while we 'fly' or 'drive' spoonfuls of nutritious food into their mouths. We want to be the best parents we can possibly be. It really is hard work trying to raise our child to be safe, healthy and sociable, isn't it?

The development of empathy

Look at your list again; have you noted that you would like your toddler to grow up to be thoughtful, kind, caring, understanding, empathic, warm or something similar? How do you think toddlers learn the skill of what is effectively empathy (though you may have given it another name)? In the next chapter we will discuss child brain development and will cover the theme of empathy from a scientific perspective. We know that empathy is a skill children learn, rather than something that is necessarily innate, and the chances are that being kind and understanding of others is something that features highly on every parent's wishes for their child. As parents we often focus on teaching our child to be empathic by reprimanding them with comments such as 'Don't do that, you'll make Johnny sad' or 'It's mean to say nasty things about people' when they do or say something that is upsetting to others; indeed it is important for them to understand that their actions can have consequences when it comes to another's feelings. We also point out feelings in others, perhaps through picture books, television programmes or plays. Whether we realise it or not we spend a lot of time each day teaching our children to be empathic.

There is a lot more to the development of empathy though and perhaps the best and indeed easiest way to teach a child to develop empathy is to be empathic to them. It seems obvious doesn't it? US President Barack Obama has spoken about what he terms society's 'Empathy Deficit': 'We live in a culture that discourages empathy. A culture that too often tells us our principal goal in life is to be rich, thin, young, famous, safe, and entertained. A culture where those in power too often encourage these selfish impulses.' You only need look at the level of hatred and crime in our society today to see the shocking evidence of this empathy deficit. Research[1] shows us that if a child's emotional needs are met at home they are more likely to develop a strong sense of empathy when they grow older and that toddlers who have a secure attachment to their parents are more caring towards others.[2]

In short, the best way to encourage our children to be empathic, to be kind, thoughtful, understanding of and gentle towards others is to treat them with the same compassion. This means listening to our children, encouraging them to share their feelings with us, being comfortable with them showing their distress, helping them to handle their feelings and meeting their emotional needs wherever possible. It means understanding that some of a toddler's most annoying traits, where we might punish them by putting them on naughty steps or in time out, such as public temper tantrums, or meltdowns when they don't want to go to nursery or get dressed in the morning, are the very traits that we should treat with respect and empathy ourselves. It means if your toddler is scared of the dark or the monsters in his room, or is reluctant to use his potty, that we listen to him, rather than ignoring his needs by forcing him to keep them inside in order to receive a sticker on his chart or a marble in his jar. We will discuss the use of common toddler behavioural strategies in some depth in chapter 5. For now I would just like to plant a small seed of thought in your mind, the idea that the most well-meant parenting methods are anything but empathic to our children and unless we show them empathy how do we expect them to be empathic towards others? This brings to mind a quote from one of my favourite books: 'You never really understand a person until you consider things from his point of view, until you climb inside of his skin and walk around in it' (Atticus Finch in *To Kill a Mockingbird*). Could empathy for our children be the key to not only surviving, but also enjoying the toddler years?

The development of confidence and independence

Look back at your list; have you noted that you would like your child to be independent, a free spirit, confident or something similar? Certainly many parents struggle with encouraging confidence and independence in their toddlers, especially when they start nursery, kindergarten or preschool. I don't think there is a parent anywhere who hasn't experienced their toddler crying and clinging to them at drop-off time and have perhaps been encouraged to leave by staff and other parents, with notions of 'he has to learn, it's for his own good'. Often when you collect them they are covered in stickers that say things like 'good boy' or 'I was good today'. All children have different needs; some children need us more, some need us less and their needs can change day to day too depending on many other factors of their life. If your child needs you is it really for his own good to leave him? What would he learn from being left sobbing and getting a sticker? What would he learn if we respected his feelings and postponed nursery for a while, perhaps just for a day, a week or perhaps more, until he felt ready to leave you confidently? Which response would be likely to lead to true independence and confidence? As psychotherapist Sue Gerhardt, author of *Why Love Matters*, comments, 'Babies need to be with people they are attached to well beyond nine months ... The first two or three years are the crucial window when various systems which manage emotions are put into place. In particular, it is when we learn to exercise self-control and to be aware of other people's needs. Without these basic emotional skills children may not grow up emotionally competent.'

I know for many this is unrealistic, particularly if you work and need to leave your child at day care. You can, however, still be empathic and consider your child's needs, and in chapter 14 we will work through an example of a child reluctant to be left in day care and I will suggest some tips to help both of you. I always come back to the idea that before independence there must always be dependence. This idea is so nicely summed up by Deborah Jackson in her book, *Three in a Bed*, 'every child is different, but his needs are universal. All he wants is the nurture of a mother – and given in sufficient quantity, at an early enough age, he will grow up with security, and with responsibility for himself.' Could allowing your child a little more dependence on you be the key for finding peace in the toddler years?

The development of curiosity and a desire to learn

Back to your list again, did you mention that you would like your child to grow into an adult who loved learning, was inquisitive, interested in the world, a free thinker with a mind of his own?

These are certainly very positive traits, which most parents would wish for their children. I remember a time when I caught my daughter, then two, having emptied a whole shelf of my kitchen larder. She had tipped half of the salt container onto the floor and then crumbled a whole packet of stock cubes on top of the salt; she had then poured most of a bottle of vinegar into the mix and was busy stirring the mixture with a teaspoon and using an upturned cup to make patterns. Then there was the time she covered herself and our living room rug with a whole tube of thick white sticky sun cream, or when she found my make-up bag and used my expensive cosmetics to draw all over herself, the mirror, the wall and the floor. Upon finding her each time I took a sharp intake of breath and my first reaction was to shout at her, but something made me pause. Had she really been so naughty? What she had done was unacceptable, yes, and I made sure it couldn't happen again by putting things away more carefully out of her reach. I also explained in each case why what she had done wasn't acceptable and offered an alternative, but similar, acceptable activity, I am not a permissive parent by any means.

Why was I not angry with her? Well, what had she done wrong? In each case she was being inquisitive and interested in the world; she was learning more than a science class could teach her, about the properties of liquids and solids, she was learning about shapes and pattern making, she was honing her fine co-ordination skills and this was all self-led, and when you think of it that way a toddler's constant drive to learn and explore their world can only be a good thing. When I thought of it another way I realised she was exploring and learning or being what we will refer to in later chapters as a 'little scientist'. Granted I would have much preferred her to play in a sandpit, to play with her pouring cups in the bath and paint at the table with lots of newspaper underneath her canvas, but the basic instinctive drive was still the same and really it was my fault for not supervising her adequately or putting items I did not want her to play with out of her reach.

Similarly, one of my children (I won't say which one for fear they or, worse, their friends, will read this book when they are older) used to 'paint' with their poo. Many a time I walked into the nursery after the morning nap to find a naked toddler, a full open nappy on the floor and a child finger-painting on the walls with poo. Again, I could have interpreted this as my child being a monster, doing things deliberately to wind me up and being 'naughty', indeed many would. Yet what this really indicated was simply a toddler who enjoyed exploring the texture of warm, sticky poo, marvelling at its paint-like properties and ability literally to stick to anything! Even better that it was something they had produced all by themselves; imagine the pride! What did I do? I resigned myself to cleaning, a lot, and we got through an awful lot of bleach in a short period of time. We learnt to put nappies and pyjamas on back to front and fix the nappy with gaffer tape; I also invested in some play dough and some paints, realising the behaviour might indicate a need for more 'messy play'. Eventually, the poo painting stopped, much to my relief!

Why do we praise an inquisitive mind so much when children are older? Why do we applaud the 'thinkers' of society and hold scientific researchers in such high esteem when we chastise and discipline our toddlers for doing the very same thing? As John Holt, author and educator, has said, 'Children are born passionately eager to make as much sense as they can of things around them. If we attempt to control, manipulate, or divert this process, the independent scientist in the child disappears.'

What if we understood their need to explore and experiment? What if we encouraged it (in ways that were acceptable to us)? Could allowing your child a little more freedom to explore the world be the key for calmness throughout toddlerdom?

The development of commitment and ambition

Looking at your list once more, did you write that you hoped your toddler would grow into a determined, ambitious, focused adult who is not afraid of commitment or hard work? Or something similar? These are all very positive traits, particularly when it comes to employment and relationships in adults. However, if you are a stubborn toddler, a wilful two-year-old or headstrong eighteen-month-old they are deemed negative behavioural traits. Why the difference in regard? Why is it acceptable and applauded to be a focused, determined, ambitious adult and yet the very same qualities are punished if you are a two-year-old?

Think how much determination your toddler requires every day; most things are too high for them, they struggle to reach, they fall over often and must pick themselves up over and over again, their fine motor skills are not yet fully developed and the jigsaw puzzle and shape sorter that is so simple for us is so challenging for them, their language skills are not yet mature enough to be fully understood all of the time, but they persist, until they have mastered the task at hand. We often don't think about quite how much commitment it takes to be a toddler and what an amazing quality their urge for mastery is. Imagine if they gave up, if they no longer bothered to learn to run, jump and climb, if they gave up on drawing because their pictures did not look like yours, or they gave up trying to speak to us because they were not understood. However would they learn? How would they develop?

Now think about your obstinate little bundle of rage refusing to put his coat on (perhaps because he is not cold and does not want to overheat or perhaps just because today he doesn't like the colour), his protestations lasting for an easy ten minutes, why doesn't he just give up and let you put his coat on? We don't realise that this stubborn behaviour that we despair of so commonly in toddlers is one of the very qualities they need to help them to grow into a successful child and adult. What if we applauded our toddler's determination to complete a task? (With appropriate limits in place.) Could affording your child a little more respect for their tenacity be the key for turning the 'terrible twos' into the 'terrific twos'?

I hope you see where I am leading you. If we think about our long term goals for our children we realise that many of them are at odds with how we may be parenting our toddlers today. Common behavioural strategies and techniques oppress many of the natural skills toddlers possess that lead to the very qualities we hope they will possess when they are older. It may be hard parenting a toddler, but it is so much harder to **be** a toddler.

The goals of the modern day parenting expert

Have you ever wondered why so many famous parenting experts tend to have worked as nannies? Consider the aims that they have in their professional capacity, either when they work in a family's home or write a toddler training manual. Their aims surely must be: 1. To do their job and be worthy of their fee; 2. To get good results, which means extinction of the undesirable behaviour; 3. To get results as quickly as possible; 4. To restore peace to the household. I believe these experts are well meaning and they do their job well, but their job focuses very much on the 'now'. It is incredibly results based, but the results are only focusing on the short term. Getting a child sleeping through the night, eating their greens, being kind to their siblings and no longer throwing a tantrum on every shopping trip are all things these parenting experts can seemingly do with ease, and their results are often very quick and seemingly very impressive. They have done their job, they have earned their fee, and they have solved the problem. Then it is time to move on to the next family and the next job.

However, it is worth considering the possible long term effects of their actions and advice. Do they have in mind the future adult that the child will be? Do they worry that these methods will inhibit the child from developing the qualities their parents so desire them to possess when they are older? Of course they don't. Many popular parenting experts, who base their work on the ideas of the behaviourists, whose theories are responsible for modern day dog training, focus only on today, rather than looking forward to who your child will become in twenty years' time. The bigger picture does not concern them, as they leave and move on to 'fixing' the next family. This is at odds with what a parent wants and hopes for their child in the long term. The question to be asked is whether it is possible to find a way to consider the long term implications of our actions while remaining sane in the present. Sometimes today is so stressful it is hard to even contemplate tomorrow isn't it? Is it possible to be mindful of tomorrow while surviving today? I think so and this is precisely what the rest of this book is all about.

Chapter 2

Why toddlers are not mini adults

Your kids require you most of all to love them for who they are, not to spend your whole time trying to correct them.

Bill Ayers, education theorist

Have you ever wondered why your toddler just doesn't seem to understand you, even if you repeat yourself one hundred times? Or why they refuse to share their toys even when their playmate is in floods of tears and you've asked really nicely? Have you ever felt they were behaving in a certain way to deliberately wind you up and wondered what you did so wrong to raise such a selfish child? The simple answer is that toddlers' brains are not like those of adults and they simply do not think in the same way that we do. With this in mind then it becomes obvious that we should not treat them as mini adults or expect them to act in the same way as us.

Many common toddler behavioural techniques do not appear to take account of paediatric neuropsychology. If they did they would surely advocate different methods. Perhaps one of the most important things a parent can understand is how their toddler's brain works. Once you understand some basic premises, your expectations of your toddler dramatically change and so too day-to-day life as a family becomes much calmer.

The nature versus nurture debate

The debate of whether behaviour is learnt or inherited has been around for centuries. Indeed the seventeenth-century English philosopher John Locke is famous for saying the following: 'The little and almost insensible impressions on our tender infancies have very important and lasting consequences.' Locke believed that newborn babies were like blank slates (or what he termed '*tabula rasa*') at birth and that their experiences of the world from birth onwards would shape their adult personalities. Locke believed that the early experiences and markings on the *tabula rasa* were much more important than the experiences and learnings of adulthood. Many supporters of the nature hypothesis cite famous twin studies to counteract the nurture hypothesis, arguing that a large amount of human behaviour is innate, an inherited trait; however, these studies have come under criticism for their small sample sizes, results that are difficult to quantify and overestimated conclusions.

In contrast to the frequently cited twin studies, the Human Genome Project, completed in 2003, seems to back up Locke's beliefs and the beliefs of those who favour the nurture view. The project predicted that there are somewhere between 20,000 and 25,000 human genomes, which means that there are quite simply not enough genomes to account for all facets of human behaviour as a hereditary trait. Or as American biologist Craig Venter, who was one of the first to sequence the human genome, says, 'The wonderful diversity of the human species is not hard-wired in our genetic code. Our environments are critical.' The nurture debate definitely wins out for me when considering many facets of toddler behaviour, though that is not to say that biology does not come into play, of course it does, which is why I believe a good basic knowledge of brain development is vital to help unravel our understanding of our young offspring and to grasp how important the first three years of life are when considering future personalities.

How does the brain develop?

A child's brain almost doubles in size over the first year of life. At birth most of the baby's brain cells are formed, however most of the hundred billion connections between the cells are made during early childhood. These connections are enormously influenced by the baby's and toddler's environment. A child's brain growth does not follow a biologically predetermined path; early experiences will interact with their genetic make-up and have an enormous impact on the development of their brain by influencing how the pathways of their brain become connected. In short, no two brains develop the same, even those of identical twins.

A toddler's brain is incredibly active: a three-year-old's brain is approximately twice as active as that of an adult and will have formed about one thousand trillion connections, again about twice as many as an adult. A young child experiences the world in a more complete, multi-sensory way than they will during the rest of their life. This means the child's development, including social, emotional, cognitive, physical and language, is stimulated during multi-sensory experiences. Mindful of this we should understand that young children need the opportunity to participate in a world filled with as many stimulating sights, sounds, feels and smells as possible.

The brain of a child will retain this enormous amount of neural connections until they reach the age of ten or eleven. From this point onwards their brain will begin to prune the extra, unused, connections, operating on a 'use it or lose it' principle. If a connection is reinforced by being used repeatedly in the early years of the child's life it becomes permanent; if the connection is not reinforced it is pruned away for ever. This means that a lack of appropriate stimulation or care at certain times in the child's life can have serious and permanent effects; this is what scientists term 'neuroplasticity' or the ability of the brain to change in response to the individual's environment. With this information in mind we can see that what happens in the child's early years is hugely influenced by their babyhood and toddlerdom and this in turn can influence the rest of their lives. Indeed, recent research[3] looking at the environment and parental nurturance received by young children shows it has a marked effect on brain development in the teenage years, with lead researcher Dr Martha Farah commenting, 'It really does support the idea that those early years are especially influential.'

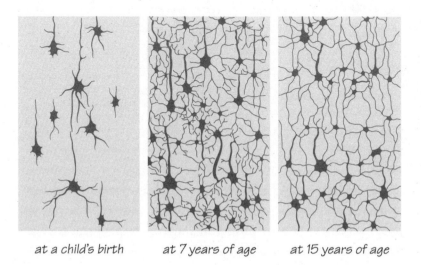

at a child's birth   *at 7 years of age*   *at 15 years of age*

The triune brain theory

I like to use the theory of the triune brain when explaining brain development to parents. This simple theory developed by American neuroscientist Paul MacLean is a wonderful way to understand brain function and development. As you might have guessed from the name (triune meaning 'three in one') the triune brain theory describes the brain as of three main parts, each part interacting with the other. These are the reptilian brain (or the reptilian cortex), the mammalian brain (the limbic system) and the thinking brain (the neocortex).

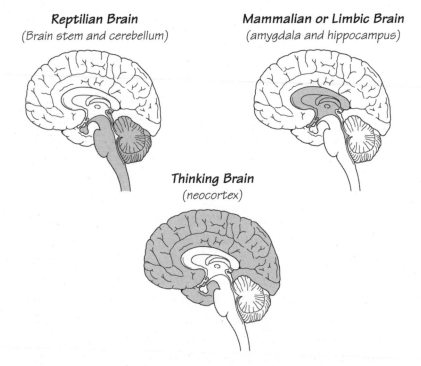

Reptilian Brain
(Brain stem and cerebellum)

Mammalian or Limbic Brain
(amygdala and hippocampus)

Thinking Brain
(neocortex)

The reptilian brain is the part of the brain necessary for basic survival and consists of the brain stem and cerebellum; it controls our essential bodily functions such as breathing, digestion, temperature regulation, circulation, hunger and thirst. The functions of the reptilian brain are automatic. This area is well developed and active from birth.

The mammalian or limbic brain, containing the amygdala and hippocampus, is the seat of emotions, giving us the capacity to feel and give love. The mammalian brain is also well developed at birth.

The thinking brain is the neocortex (literally meaning 'new brain'); it makes up approximately five-sixths of the human brain. The size of our neocortex is what sets us apart from our Neanderthal ancestors and distinguishes us from other mammals. The neocortex is the seat of critical and rational thought, or what many perceive to be 'intelligence', as well as the home of voluntary movement. Development of the neocortex is not well under way until a child reaches approximately the age of four years.

With this understanding of brain development we can see how social development such as empathy, self-awareness and the ability to interact with others, all functions of the neocortex, does not really develop until a child reaches almost school age. This means that children lack the social development necessary to share until around the age of four onwards. This is such an important point I feel I need to say it twice: toddlers and most preschoolers are physically incapable of sharing; their brains are not developed enough to do the very thing we try so hard to teach them to do on an almost daily basis.

The neocortex is also the home of impulse control and the ability to understand that a choice we make now may have consequences later. Neuroscientists tell us that toddlers are incapable of controlling their impulses and their 'big emotions', which is why they tantrum with such ferocity. They do not do so to manipulate or annoy us deliberately; they can't help it! Toddlers do not have the brain development necessary to stay in control of their feelings and they do not understand the use of consequences, such as 'If you do that again I'll take the toy away from you' as a punishment. Wow.

Remember I mentioned earlier that the neocortex is also the home of empathy as well as our abilities to use reason and logic. The neocortex is the last part of the triune brain to form and is therefore not mature in toddlers. A toddler simply does not have the neural connections necessary to understand logic and reasoning, no matter how much you explain to them logically why it is inappropriate to wear shorts on a winter's day or nothing more than wellington boots and a tutu to preschool.

Why then do we have such incorrect expectations of toddlers? Why do we get angry when they don't listen to our logical commands, share their toys, fail to see how another person feels and scream at the top of their lungs at the supermarket? If we understand some basic neuropsychology we understand these behaviours are totally **normal** for toddlers. We accept that toddlers have a limited ability to talk, yet we don't constantly punish them for not speaking in long, complex sentences, so why don't we accept their other biological limitations too? The only answer I can come up with is that most people simply don't know that this behaviour is normal.

The egocentric toddler

Many years ago, before the advent of complex imaging machinery, we had already reached the conclusion that young children think and feel differently to adults. Perhaps the most influential researcher in the field of child development was Jean Piaget, a Swiss philosopher and psychologist, credited with being the founding father of developmental psychology. Piaget was famous for suggesting that children move from a state of egocentrism (categorised by 'incomplete differentiation of the self and the world and other people' – thinking that everyone in the world thinks, feels and sees things the same as them) to sociocentrism at around the age of seven. In other words he suggests that it takes them around seven years until they finally recognise that others see the world in a different way to them. Piaget's work helps us to understand that an egocentric child is not a selfish child, but rather one who is too young to have learnt that others may have different beliefs and opinions to them. This has enormous implications as it literally highlights to us that young children are incapable of having true empathy for others.

The 'three mountains' experiment

Piaget used a number of creative experiments to study the mental abilities of children, paying particular attention to the concept of egocentrism. Perhaps the most famous of these experiments is known as the 'three mountains'. Piaget's technique for studying egocentrism involved using a three-dimensional model of a mountain scene. In the experiment young children were asked to choose a picture that showed the scene they had just seen. Most children could to do this with little difficulty.

In the next part of the experiment the children were asked to select a picture showing what another person would have seen when looking at the mountain from a different viewpoint. Unsurprisingly the young children almost always chose the scene showing their own view of the mountains. Children experience this difficulty because they are unable to take on another person's perspective, or what Piaget termed egocentrism. How do you think this might relate to us as parents when we are lecturing our toddlers about how another person feels? Or telling them to apologise for something such as 'stealing' a toy? When you know that your toddler's mental abilities do not allow him to understand the point of view of others, should your expectations change?

Toddlers are little scientists

Piaget also identified a developmental stage where toddlers act as 'little scientists', constantly trying new things to get results through trial and error experiments. One such example of this might be an eighteen-month-old seated in his highchair who constantly throws his beaker to the floor. To us it is a nuisance, but to the child he is learning that 'If I throw my beaker from my highchair Mum makes a funny shrieking sound and picks it up again'. How clever is he?

Piaget termed the mental and physical actions involved in understanding and knowing 'schemas'.

Piaget saw a schema as including certain knowledge as well as the process of obtaining that knowledge and stated that as the child had new experiences then the new information would be used to modify, add to or change previously existing schemas. An example of a schema would be if a child had a pet cat that had black fur and green eyes. Originally he may believe that all cats have black fur and green eyes, but if he saw a new cat, perhaps a tabby cat with orange eyes, he would absorb the new information and modify his previously existing 'cat schema' to include this new information. Experimentation is a vital component of the development of schemas and we could say schemas are how a toddler makes sense of the world.

Monkey see, monkey do

Psychologist Albert Bandura's work on social learning theory is also useful to consider here. Bandura's research in the 1960s studied the foundations of human learning by analysing the ability of children to imitate behaviour observed in others. Perhaps Bandura's most famous experiment is that of the 'Bobo doll' (the Bobo doll being a sort of inflatable clown). This research shows clearly that children imitate and learn from the world around them.

Bandura's Bobo doll experiment involved assigning children into one of three groups: 1. Aggressive modelling; half same-sex adult pairing, half different; 2. Non-aggressive modelling; half same-sex adult pairing, half different; and 3. The control group.

The children in the experiment were led into a room with their assigned adult: one side of the room contained toys for children; the other side held items for the adult – a hammer, the Bobo doll and some small toys. The children were specifically told 'Do not touch the adult toys'. In the aggressive group the adult hit the Bobo doll (with their hands and the hammer); while in the non-aggressive group the adult just played with the small toys and ignored the Bobo doll. After ten minutes the child was removed from the room.

The child was then taken to a new room with lots of interesting toys, but after two minutes the children were told they were no longer allowed the toys (this was done in order to raise frustration levels), but they could play with the toys in the experiment room. The children were then led back into the original room. While the child was back in the experiment room they were observed for how many times they were violent to the Bobo doll, how many times they were verbally violent and how many times they were violent with the hammer.

Unsurprisingly, Bandura found that the children exposed to the aggressive model, that is the adult who hit the Bobo doll, were more likely to be physically aggressive than those who were not exposed to the aggressive model. Interestingly he also found that boys were three times more likely to be violent than girls. Bandura also concluded that children are more influenced by same-sex models. In summary, Bandura's simple experiment taught us that children model our actions, both good and bad. If we are violent towards them, so we increase the chances of them being violent towards others. If they bite us and we bite them back we are doing nothing but affirming their action that violence is acceptable; similarly if we smack them we show them it is OK to hit others.

In case you're feeling a little wrung out with all of the science talk I'd like to introduce you to a simple metaphor, which I have found helpful.

Toddlers are like bungalows

We know now that a toddler's brain is very different to that of an adult; they are not 'mini adults' and so should not be treated as such. Toddlers do not think like us or feel like us, therefore a different way of communicating with them is necessary. Take for instance a two-year-old girl, whose brain structure is hugely different to that of a woman. Her neocortex, the thinking, analytical, rational, frontal part of her brain, is grossly under-developed in comparison to its future state.

Inspired by an idea discussed by Professor of Psychiatry Dr

Dan Siegel, I'd like to use the following metaphor to explain this concept. Imagine the little girl's brain is like a single-storey, one-bedroom bungalow. It has a kitchen stocked with food, a bathroom and a sofa bed, indeed everything she needs for her basic survival, but nothing spare for anything more; it is lacking the first floor of a two-storey house, like that of an adult.

The two-storey adult brain has all the toddler's brain has, with those rooms that encompass the basic needs for survival, but the added first floor provides a whole lot more. The first floor in the adult house provides a study, a place for contemplation and a bedroom suite, a place for calmness and relaxation, in which hangs a large mirror, for self-reflection and the development of empathy.

In the bungalow when the toddler is scared her emotions swirl around the rooms like smoke, but sometimes, in fact lots of times, the feelings (the smoke) become overwhelming and without a first storey to diffuse them through the air purifier in the contemplation room, they literally 'flip out' and escape easily, just like smoke from an open fire escaping through a chimney. In an adult house, though, any big feelings originating downstairs in the primal part of their 'home' can move upstairs where they can be diffused and rational decisions made. Adults therefore no longer need to tantrum, their house contains everything they need in order to manage their emotions, or should I say at least that is the case for most adults, for we all know an adult who has little self-control, over their anger for instance, and most likely the reasons can be traced back to their own formative years.

Toddlers do not have this sophisticated second storey to their homes, just like the lack of a well-developed neocortex in their brains, they do not have extra 'rooms' to diffuse their feelings, they do not have 'rooms' of contemplation and rational thought, they do not have a mirror to reflect on the feelings of others in order to understand the concept of empathy, yet they are not selfish; they just cannot comprehend that other people may have different feelings to them.

Toddlers and preschoolers have raw emotions, big feelings and no other way of dealing with them other than letting go or 'flipping out'. As parents I believe it is our role to understand this and to understand that young children need our help to handle their big feelings. When we help them through these feelings, instead of forcing them to bury them in the murky depths of their basements, where they will sit and fester, likely to cause future problems, then we are truly giving them the best opportunity to develop well.

To continue the metaphor, just as it takes builders a while to add a second storey to a house, so too it takes the architects and builders of a young child's brain time to form the connections, to join the bricks you might say, for the next 'layer' of their brain. Under the age of five children definitely live in bungalows; in fact it can take right up to the teenage years for their extension to be fully completed and habitable. That's not all though. During childhood the way we treat our children can have a lasting effect on the structure of their brain, the way we treat them almost forms the architectural plans for their second storey. If we treat them with empathy and compassion, listen to them, honour their feelings and help them to feel validated, accepted and unconditionally loved, then the second storey will almost always go well. The plans will lead to well-built walls that will see them through for the rest of their lives. In short their 'home' will be a good place for them to live for many years to come, equipping them with all that they need.

Yet what happens if we do not treat our children with compassion? What if we punish them, yell at them, shut them in their rooms, leave them in 'time out' or on the naughty step, teach them that our love is conditional, that they aren't 'good enough', that they must cope with their fears and big emotions alone, especially at night when we would rather sleep than help them to diffuse their fear or loneliness, because their feelings are uncomfortable and unacceptable to us?

When we think of toddlers in this way, not only do we see with clarity how to help them achieve the qualities we would like them to possess as an adult, the very same ones you noted in chapter 1, we also understand why our actions today will have a lasting effect on their well-being tomorrow. This knowledge that our toddler's behaviour is **normal** and healthy for a child of their age can also make them much easier to live with, particularly when paired with the knowledge that this tricky period of development won't last for ever!

I'd like to end this chapter by introducing you to Jo and her 'little scientist' master explorer daughter Neve.

Jo's story

When my daughter Neve was nearly three we started the process of potty training. We left her a pink princess toilet seat in the bathroom ready for her to use whenever she wanted to. One Friday morning I heard a shout from the bathroom 'Mummy I'm stuck'. I went in to find that Neve had put her head through her little toilet seat. 'Come here, sweetheart,' I said as I went to pull it straight off, only to discover it didn't want to go over her ears. I decided I would have another go at removing it downstairs where her baby brother was waiting not so patiently for his breakfast.

Once in the living room no amount of jiggling the seat around could get it over her ears; the baby was crying with hunger and hearing her brother crying was upsetting Neve even more. In an attempt to calm the situation I popped the telly on for Neve and gave her some toast, hoping that she would sit still watching the children's programmes and not be in too much discomfort while I fed the baby his breakfast. I planned to tackle her again with lots of moisturiser on her ears once both kids had contentedly full tummies.

My plan didn't exactly work as I'd hoped, though. It seemed Neve had been busy exploring her own ways of freeing herself while I fed her brother. As I turned around I saw she had managed to thread one arm through the toilet seat, meaning it was now around her body and over her shoulder, diagonally around her chest. Realising that I was now going to need to enlist help to remove the seat I ran through my options. My husband would still be driving on his way to work so would not answer his phone and all three of us were still in our pyjamas so I didn't want to go and knock on the door of our neighbour two houses down, who is generally very 'handy', but I didn't have his phone number. So I settled for ringing the lady who lives next door, but she had just put a tint on her hair so was also housebound. She also informed me that the helpful chap two doors down was away.

At this point Neve was still OK, but rapidly getting bored with the situation. Despite the fact that she had managed to pull the toilet seat on with relative ease during her explorations, I could now see that there was no way it was going to be removed other than by being cut off. I rang a friend to see if her husband had any tools that might help but drew a blank, so I started to wonder about calling the fire brigade. I knew they'd have something with which to cut it off, and the fire station was literally around the corner from my house. I called the local number and without further ado I was told the patrol team were on their way and they reassured me I had done the right thing in calling them.

Now, toddlers are not known for their sense of timing and Neve proceeded to do a big smelly poo in her nappy just before they arrived. She wouldn't let me change it as she was fed up with me man-handling her by this time, so when the fire brigade arrived I found myself apologising for the smell as well as the predicament. The small living room of the cottage soon felt very full with two firemen in it, wearing full kit and big jackets, then to top it off when fireman no. 3 walked in, Neve declared 'It's, Amelie's daddy!' I could have died with embarrassment as the father of one of Neve's preschool class-mates entered the room. This did however turn out to be a bonus as he volunteered to entertain the baby as I held Neve, while the other two firemen very carefully cut her out.

Incidentally, they said they had been called to a similar sit-uation in the past, but it was the child's bottom that was stuck in the seat. Neve continues to explore the world around her; I just hope that her adventures don't result in another call to the fire service!

Chapter 3

The science
of toddler sleep

I sometimes wake in the early morning and listen to the soft breathing of my child and I think to myself, this is one thing I will never regret and I carry that quiet with me all day long.

Brian Andreas, artist and storyteller

I think most parents expect sleepless nights with a newborn baby, as heaven knows enough people warn you about 'what you've got coming' when you're expecting. Naively, though, many parents, myself included, are under the mistaken belief that the sleepless nights end somewhere around the middle of your baby's first year. It is an unpleasant shock then to realise that for the majority of families this is simply not the case. Toddlers wake regularly throughout the night, they wake early in the morning and horrifyingly they begin to drop their daytime naps when you most need them to have them, often when you are expecting a new baby sibling. Throw nightmares, night terrors, night-time potty training and bed wetting into the mix and toddler sleep can sometimes be harder to handle than the sleepless nights of babyhood.

The norms of toddler sleep

Research conducted in 2012[4] highlights quite clearly how normal it is for toddlers to wake regularly at night. With findings showing that around one-third of 1,200 infants studied still woke at night at least twice per week at the age of fifteen months and once per week by the time they were two years old. These findings back up earlier research,[5] which shows us that at the age of one 40 per cent of toddlers wake and need their parents' help in order to go back to sleep. Another large-scale study[6] conducted on over 3,000 Australian children highlights again that nighttime waking is common in the toddler years with a third of all parents considering their toddler's sleep 'problematic' and regular night waking, requiring attention, becoming less common only after the child has turned two years of age. This research also indicated that settling back to sleep requires more parental input from eighteen months of age onwards: this increased need for our help at night is usually attributed to the fact that toddlers have to cope with increasing levels of significant developmental issues, such as autonomy (the freedom to act independently), increased amounts of separation from parents, often through day care, preschool and kindergarten and object permanence (the knowledge that something is still present when it is out of sight).

Circadian rhythms and REM sleep maturation

One huge difference between the biology of a toddler and an adult is in the maturity of their circadian rhythms, or what we more commonly refer to as our 'body clocks'. Circadian rhythms are the body's own natural twenty-four-hourly sleep/wake cycle, controlled through the hormones melatonin and cortisol, and their response to daylight viewed through our eyes. Melatonin is a hormone that makes us sleepy, release is triggered by dim light and levels therefore peak in the evening and at night. Levels of cortisol, a hormone that makes us alert, on the other hand, are at their highest levels around thirty minutes after waking each morning, levels then gradually decline throughout the course of the day.[7] When your toddler was *in utero* he borrowed the maternal circadian rhythms,[8] passed to him via the placenta. After birth, however, and the cutting of the umbilical cord he was on his own. An infant's circadian rhythms take time to mature and they are not fully comparable to that of an adult until preschool age, with research[9] showing cortisol levels developing a more adult-like pattern of release throughout the toddler years, with the researchers quoting '... it [circadian rhythm] attains complete maturity, guaranteeing a similar response to adult behaviour, from one year onwards. What is important to emphasise is that, most probably, there are no fixed dates for expression of the circadian activity ... In fact, this period is moveable, being dependent on variations in the environmental characteristics and the habits of specific populations.'

Cortisol levels can also be affected by the toddler's environment and research[10,11,12] suggests that they may be elevated in the afternoons when a child is in a day care setting, whereas for a toddler in a home environment the levels decrease. This means that a toddler in day care, with elevated cortisol levels, will need a longer period of wind-down time once they arrive home so that their cortisol levels can lower enough for restful sleep. Sadly this is often at odds with parents' schedules, particularly if they both work late and don't arrive home with their toddlers until 6pm or even later, and then are keen to move through the dinner, bath and bed routine in order to maintain some of their adult evening time. In this case the toddler is unlikely to be ready to sleep until 8pm or even later.

In a similar vein research has found that television viewing significantly increased the incidence of sleep disturbances in five-to six-year-olds. The researchers concluded that 'The results suggest that health-care professionals should be aware of the association between TV exposure and sleep disturbances'. For this reason I also suggest limiting television exposure in the evenings with absolutely no screen time in the hour before bed and preferably the two hours before bedtime.

Another difference between toddler and adult sleep is the length of REM sleep experienced. REM or rapid eye movement sleep is also known as 'active sleep'. In this sleep state our brains are active and our body is immobile, while our breathing and heart rate is relatively irregular. REM sleep is the host to dreams and nightmares and also the state of sleep we are most likely to awaken from. Young babies spend 50 per cent of their total sleep duration in this state, which decreases to around 30 per cent in early toddlerhood and further decreases to 25 per cent by the age of five. By the time we reach adulthood REM sleep accounts for around 22 per cent of our total sleep. This shows that a toddler spends around 25 per cent more time each night in a lighter sleep state than an adult does, giving them many more opportunities to awaken, especially if you consider that this sleep state is the state in which nightmares occur. If a child has more vivid dreams than an adult it is only natural that they may wake and cry out more often, due to fear and anxiety.

Night terrors and nightmares

Night terrors are possibly one of the most alarming things to witness as a parent. My eldest son suffered badly with night terrors when he was around three years old. He used to cry out at night like a wounded animal; his eyes would be open, but they were glazed, which indicated he was not really awake, he used to thrash around uncontrollably; sobbing all the while he did so. Nothing we did helped or soothed him and many times he would accidentally hit us. The only thing we found that helped was time: eventually he would calm down and appear to sleep soundly again and he would never remember the event in the morning. He eventually grew out of them after a period of about six months.

Night terrors occur most commonly between the ages of two and five years old, but it is not unknown for them to happen earlier. Boys tend to be more affected than girls and they are more likely to occur during times of stress or extreme tiredness. As I have already mentioned night terrors tend to be extremely distressing for the parents, but they are generally self-limiting both in duration and in the period of time over which the toddler experiences them.

During a night terror, although it might seem as if the child is awake and hallucinating, they are actually very much asleep. Night terrors occur during a phase of sleep known as stage 3–4 NREM, or non-rapid eye movement sleep. This phase of sleep is characterised as deep sleep where it is extremely difficult to arouse the child and if aroused from this phase of sleep the toddler is likely to be disorientated for a few minutes. Because night terrors occur in such a deep sleep state the toddler is left with no memory of the event.

Nightmares on the other hand occur during REM sleep, a light sleep state where it is very easy to arouse the toddler into a waking state. Disorientation should be minimal here when compared to arousal from NREM sleep and when the child wakes they are likely to have a memory of the nightmare.

Unfortunately there is not a great deal that you can do when your toddler experiences a night terror, aside from trying to alleviate any known stress from the child's environment, trying to ensure that he gets enough sleep and trying to keep him safe during an event. Some parents report a reduction in night terrors using a process of scheduled awakenings first introduced by psychiatrist Bryan Lask at Great Ormond Street Hospital in 1988. In this process parents begin by keeping a diary of the times that their child's night terrors occur over several nights. If a pattern emerges they are advised to wake the child around ten to fifteen minutes before the night terrors usually occur, and then they should try to keep them awake for five minutes before allowing them to go back to sleep again.

The controlled crying myth

The act of leaving toddlers to cry for a predetermined period of time in order to teach them to fall asleep by themselves and learn the skill of 'self-settling' is perhaps the mainstay of modern toddler sleep training with research[13] indicating that 27 per cent of parents leave their children to cry themselves to sleep. This form of sleep training has many names from 'cry it out' to 'controlled crying', 'self-soothing' to 'pick up, put down' and 'graduated extinction'. Many experts who advocate these techniques insist that they 'don't do controlled crying', when in fact they do, they just choose to give it a new, softer-sounding name. The idea of leaving infants to cry in order that they may fall asleep without adult help was introduced by Dr Emmett Holt in his 1895 book *The Care and Feeding of Children*, and this idea was further popularised by Dr Richard Ferber (which gave rise to the term 'Ferberisation') in his 1985 book *Solve Your Child's Sleep Problems*.

So does this form of sleep training work? Does controlled crying usually result in a toddler who will eventually fall asleep by himself? Yes, it usually does, though not always. How about another question: 'Does it make toddlers learn to self-soothe, develop healthy sleep habits and guarantee long-term nights of sleeping through?' The answer here is a resounding 'No'. Yet perhaps the most important question of all that a parent could ask here would be, 'Will it cause any long-term negative effects to my child's development and will the process cause them stress and trauma?' The answer here is a very loud 'Yes'.

Perhaps some of the most compelling evidence to date, concerning the potential side effects of sleep training such as controlled crying, is research conducted at the University of North Texas.[14] This simple, elegant study shows the dissonance between the popular and very much mistaken assumptions that sleep trained infants self-soothe into a state of firstly calmness and secondly sleep, and what really happens to them. In short the research clearly proved that while children may not cry out for their mother after a few nights of controlled crying, they are anything but soothed, with their spiked cortisol levels (a stress hormone) indicating the real trauma they were experiencing internally. Currently the work of those keen to show the efficacy and safety of sleep training[15,16] does not provide adequate evidence of no harm, yet the research into controlled crying and cortisol levels I have mentioned above most definitely indicates evidence of harm. Why then is it the former that is more widely reported and latched onto by worldwide health services and workers? Why do we still advocate sleep training for toddlers? Professor Middlemiss, lead researcher in the cortisol research mentioned above, joins me in her disdain of the recent flurry of researchers desperate to prove that sleep training babies and toddlers is both safe and effective, commenting that 'Parental fatigue is not generally reported with one night waking; early wakings seem to sort themselves out by the second year of life. So ... Why does research continue to focus on waking? It isn't the waking. It's the regulation of responses and the best regulation comes from attention, touch, proximity, responsiveness.'

The illusion of self-soothing

One of the myths perpetuated by the sleep training advocates is that it is important to encourage a toddler to learn how to fall asleep by themselves, or what they term 'self-soothe'. My belief, and one that is shared by psychologists all around the world, is that there is no such thing as 'self-soothing' with babies and toddlers. We already know from chapter 2 that toddlers do not have the brain development necessary to diffuse and regulate their emotions. Rather, their eventual silence and slumber after a period of 'cry it out' or 'controlled crying' is as a result of them giving up, much like infants in orphanages around the world who sit in silence, what point is there in continuing to cry if nobody comes? I cannot highlight enough that this is not self-soothing.

In order to self-soothe the child has to have the brain development necessary for rational thought, and toddlers do not. Professor Middlemiss explains more, 'Soothing is part of the self-regulatory behaviour that will develop as infants mature and as their physiological responses mature. This maturity is best achieved, according to extensive research, through attention to signalling. The adult is the first source of emotional and physiological regulation for infants. Through their guided regulation, infants develop physiological and emotional regulation. There is an extensive body of research that shows without this responsiveness, physiological and neurological development is impaired ... not supported. Thus, it is parents' early presence and guidance in regulating emotional responses for infants that is likely to contribute to infants' developing capacity to soothe themselves.'

So the real key to help your toddler learn to self-soothe, at a time when their development allows such a skill, is really to remain as responsive to them as possible now, to take care of their needs while also being mindful of your own, for the two are very much interlinked. Our responses to our toddler's totally normal night awakenings determine whether our young truly have the ability to self-soothe to sleep later in life, and by not leaving them to 'self-soothe' at a time when they are psychologically and biologically unable to, we are more likely to create a confident and independent child.

Some advice for sleep-deprived parents of toddlers

What can be done to help parents who are despairing of their offspring's (lack of) sleep? I have a few ideas:

1. Society can educate them about normal toddler sleep, which is precisely why I began this chapter in the way that I did. The effect on parents upon hearing that their baby's sleep is entirely normal never ceases to amaze me. Once we know something is normal and therefore only a problem if it is a problem for us personally it suddenly lessens hugely in intensity. I feel it is vitally important that every parent understands what real toddler sleep looks like.

2. Society can provide unbiased factual information, not only on the normality of toddler sleep, but on the pros and cons of different forms of sleep training and modification, allowing parents to make a truly informed choice. Part of this may involve challenging the voices of those 'experts' who choose to ignore the scientific evidence surrounding toddler sleep and related behavioural modifications.

3. Society can help parents to know that they are not alone, by supporting them, listening to them and nurturing them on their parenting journey so that they may nurture their toddlers in the way that they see fit.

4. Society needs to provide more practical help and more economical support in order that parents can concentrate more on raising their young children.
5. Ideally, health and childcare professionals around the world would stay up to date with current sleep research, not just that from researchers with the loudest voices and most column inches.
6. Parents should be provided with support and information in order that they may form their own toolkit to help them through the sleepless nights.

ToddlerCalm™ teachers around the world focus on most of these points with toddler sleep workshops providing a haven for tired parents to share information in a supportive environment, research different methods of sleep training and share suggestions for ways through the maze of sleepless nights. My biggest aim here is to help you to understand that your toddler's sleep is most likely entirely normal, and now we have hopefully reset your expectations of your toddler's sleep we can briefly look at some ways to help your family cope at night. I will also discuss an example of coping with toddler sleep in the CRUCIAL chapter: chapter 14.

Early waking

Many parents ask me for my help with their toddler's early morning rising and I'm sorry to say that there is no magic answer. If you have an early waker take heart in the knowledge that he will not wake early for ever; in fact very soon you will be struggling to rouse him and get him out of bed in time to get ready for school, which is usually superseded by the grunts of a sleepy teenager reluctant to rise anytime before midday. Remember I told you in my introduction that I was most definitely not a perfect parent?

My key to surviving early waking was the knowledge that one day, in the not too distant future, I would be the one breezily announcing 'Good morning' to my teenage children, opening their curtains, turning back their duvets and loudly singing a dawn chorus while they throw pillows at me with a groan of 'Muuum, go away'. That thought got me through many a tough wake-up in the wee small hours.

In all seriousness, the key to coping with early waking is to adjust your own life. If your toddler wakes you at 5am every day, consider going to bed an hour or two earlier at night yourself so that you do not feel so exhausted with your new early starts. Some people feel that blackout blinds work to buy them a few extra precious minutes or, if they are very lucky, an hour, in bed, however they are not a magic solution for everybody. I know it is small comfort knowing that early wakings are very normal, but they are, and I promise they won't last for ever.

Bedtime rituals

Research[17] into the sleep behaviour of toddlers between the ages of eighteen and thirty-six months has shown that the use of a consistent bedtime ritual, which included massaging a lotion into the toddler's skin, quiet activities such as cuddling and singing and lights out within thirty minutes of bath-time, can help to improve not only the timing of sleep onset, number of night awakenings and need for parental input at night, but also maternal mood. Lead researcher Dr Jodi Mindell, Professor of Psychology at Saint Joseph's University in Philadelphia, stated, 'There is no question that maternal mood and children's sleep impact one another. The better a child sleeps and the easier bedtime is, the better a mother's mood is going to be. In addition, a mom who is not feeling tense, depressed, and fatigued is going to be calmer at bedtime, which will help a child settle down to sleep.'

The ToddlerCalm™ three step bedtime ritual

With the research into toddler bedtime rituals in mind, I developed what I call the ToddlerCalm™ three step bedtime ritual. This is an incredibly simple bedtime routine that really does seem to have amazing effects on toddler sleep and parental stress levels.

Step 1: Expectations

We can use our understanding of behavioural sleep training and classical conditioning in order to help us to realise kinder, gentler ways of settling toddlers. Toddlers very quickly learn 'what comes next' and we can use this to our advantage. If we perform a consistent ritual every night, such as a bath, followed by a massage in a dimly lit nursery, a story and a cuddle, and then into bed, we can give our toddler not only a sense of consistency and reassurance through a known ritual, but also we allow ourselves time to unwind and create a nurturing environment in which our toddlers can feel safe and secure to sleep.

Step 2: Sleep cues

Adding cues to a bedtime ritual can be powerful sleep triggers. I like to make these cues as multi-sensory as possible, with the knowledge that toddlers experience the world in a much more sensory way than adults. My favourite cues to use are smell and sound.

For smell I use a battery operated aromatherapy fan known as an 'aromafan' with a couple of drops of calming essential oil, such as chamomile or lavender oil, each evening while the rest of the ritual is followed. This allows the toddler the chance to link the relaxing ritual and smell, with the smell providing re-assurance once the ritual has ended. I use battery operated aromafans as this means that they are safe to be left on in the nursery all night as they do not involve naked flames. They are also highly portable, and can be taken on holiday and trips away very easily, so when everything else changes for your toddler they have the constant of their 'bedtime smell'.

For sound I use calming music, preferably music that is sixty to seventy beats per minute (resting pulse rate) with elements of heartbeat sounds or white noise. At ToddlerCalm™ we have developed a special toddler relaxation CD, which really does seem to work magic when played at the same time as the bed-time ritual and relaxing smell.

Even without the ritual, once conditioned, the smells and the music become strong relaxation cues for the toddler; they need not be limited to night-time sleep either, as they are just as useful at nap time. Remember, though, that your toddler must always be conditioned first, that is don't expect the ToddlerCalm™ CD or aromatherapy oil to work magic alone; you first have to teach your toddler the link and work with the association before it becomes conditioned.

Step 3: Comforters

Many people misunderstand comforters, or lovies, as they are sometimes known, as being items for children to cuddle and calm themselves with by touch. Touch is obviously vitally impor-tant for calming toddlers (which is another reason I recommend massage as part of the bedtime ritual, for massage releases the love and bonding hormone oxytocin in both parent and toddler as well as lowering stress levels in both), but I have always believed the most important thing about comforters is the smell, and most importantly the smell of the mother. If you are happy to bedshare with your toddler at night then obviously your toddler will have no need for a comforter as he has the real thing!

In order for comforters to be effective you first need to condition your toddler to link the comforter with you. You can build this association by encouraging your toddler to hold the comforter while having cuddles with Mummy or perhaps during story time or feeding time. I quite often recommend that the mother sleeps with the comforter for a few nights, next to her skin, so that her scent may build up on it. When conditioned well, soft fabric comforters can be powerful sleep aids, not only in getting to sleep at the start of the night, but helping the toddler to go back to sleep when they wake in the night. I will discuss the use of comforters in more detail in chapter 12.

Before I end this chapter I would just like to add how important it is for toddlers to view their bedroom as a positive place to be. This means that their bedroom should never be a place of punishment, for 'time out' or similar and they should never be 'sent to their room' as a punishment. It is also a good idea to play, cuddle, read and enjoy being in the child's room together as much as possible during daylight hours too, in order to build up this positive association.

During my years of working with parents I have discussed sleep thousands of times; particularly paying attention to the expectations of toddler sleep we have today. Sometimes this information really clicks for a parent and the realisation that their toddler is normal and the problems they are experiencing with their sleep are only transient helps a parent to reset their expectations, which in turn leads to significantly less stress and upset for the whole family.

Corinne's story

My son, Isaac, slept for durations of four hours plus overnight at around eight to ten weeks of age, but from the twelve-week developmental leap onwards, periods of more than a couple of hours of unbroken sleep at a time became a distant memory. This continued with his first, then second birthday passing and his sleep not improving. I didn't count the number of wakings he had in a night; it would have been too depressing to know.

I learnt from conversations with my own mother that I was five years old when I finally slept all night, so I figured that there could well be a genetic link and resolved to be patient, believing and hoping that it would happen in time. But the waiting was hard, really hard.

When Isaac was nearly three years old I discovered, via ToddlerCalm™, that the age range for maturation of a child's circadian rhythm is somewhere between four months and four years. I cried when I heard this; it was a revelation that helped me to a greater understanding of my toddler's sleep; a vindication of my deep feeling of resistance to force him to sleep for longer durations using sleep training or night weaning; and a relaxation about whether I was a good mother, in what felt like a whole town of perfect sleepers. The information boosted my empathy for my child, my ability to be patient night after night, and my confidence in our approach to our child's night-time sleep. Now that he is four years old Isaac finally sleeps all night, in the family bed. I knew it would happen eventually.

Chapter 4

The science of picky eating

Parenting a toddler is like turning the blender on without a lid.

Unknown

For me, the hardest thing about toddler parenting was coping with picky eating. My firstborn ate brilliantly during his first year of life. He would eat every vegetable I presented to him and enjoyed all meals from cottage pie to curry, chicken stew to beef stroganoff, and he had a hearty appetite too. I used to take great pride in preparing his meals; most of the fruit and vegetables were either home grown in our garden or delivered weekly in an organic vegetable box from a local farm. I used to choose the best cuts of organic meat and fish for him and would spend hours in the kitchen lovingly preparing meals to ensure he grew strong and healthy. I was rewarded in turn by his apparent appreciation and enjoyment of food.

Then my chubby baby with the healthy appetite and

adventurous taste in food turned into a toddler and almost overnight he stopped eating. He refused the foods he had previously loved and gone was his love of vegetables; now he would only eat carrots and even then they had to be raw and cut into finger-sized sticks. The only meat he would eat was chicken and he would no longer try any variety of fish. He refused most food that wasn't white, yellow, cream or orange; the only green food that passed his lips was small quantities of cucumber. He seemed determined to live on a diet almost exclusively made up of cheese, chicken and processed carbohydrates. His appetite seemed to shrink significantly too and at dinner time it was rare that he would eat more than a couple of forkfuls of food, despite me pretending his fork was an aeroplane flying into his mouth or a steam train driving into a tunnel, complete with loud sound effects. I encouraged him to 'eat just one more mouthful for mummy', I banned all snacks and treats, I bought sticker charts and rewarded him with toys when he filled them and whenever he cleared a plate we cheered.

While this was happening I felt terrible: I felt guilty that my son wasn't eating what he needed to eat to be healthy; I felt a failure on days out with friends whose toddlers ate whatever was put in front of them; I felt angry at my son when he wouldn't eat, sometimes wondering if he was acting that way on purpose in order to manipulate me for some reason. I became totally obsessed with my son's eating, or rather lack of, and it ruled our lives for well over a year. I don't know what happened to change things; I don't think it was any one particular event, but somewhere along the line I started to accept him as he was and I learnt to accept that this was just the way he ate. I no longer fought him and I no longer made train noises to try to encourage him to eat more.

In some ways I think I felt I had given up, surrendered with no fight left in me, but looking back my acceptance of his eating habits was the key for us turning a corner. Now he is just about to start high school, and eating is still not big on his agenda, as he prefers to graze than eat a big meal and he is still not a fan of vegetables, but he is strong and healthy and right on the average height and weight for his age, and he loves exotic food, particularly Indian and Mexican, and fish features highly on his list of favourite foods. I look back now on the toddler years with regret, for wasting so much time and energy fretting over his food intake, worrying that it was somehow a reflection of my parenting abilities. I realise now that he was perfectly normal and his eating habits merely a reflection of society's misunderstanding of toddler eating rather than a problem belonging to him or me.

Whose problem is it really?

Research[18] suggests almost a quarter of parents perceive that their toddler has an eating problem. The two most common perceived problems are that toddlers eat a limited variety of foods and prefer drinks to solid food. Thirty-seven per cent of parents defined their toddlers as 'faddy eaters'. These findings left the researchers to conclude that 'Eating problems are common in toddlers and in the majority are associated with normal growth.' Could the real reason that so many parents struggle with toddler eating problems be because their toddler does not actually have an eating problem? What if it was totally normal for toddlers to be picky eaters? What if it was totally normal for toddlers to be reluctant to try new food, prefer to drink milk than eat solid food and prefer to graze on small amounts of food rather than eat 'three square meals per day'? What if the problem with our toddlers' eating behaviour is really ours and not theirs? Now there's a thought.

I need to add a small caveat here, as I know that some parents will be thinking 'But my toddler eats really well, does that mean the he has a problem because he isn't a picky eater?' and my reply to this would simply be that all toddlers are different, some love their food, some don't, usually they are all completely normal and they are most definitely all individuals.

The most common reasons for toddler eating problems

I believe the most common underlying reasons behind what we perceive as eating problems are as follows:

- incorrect expectations

- a need for control from the toddler's point of view

- biological differences in taste between adults and young children.

Incorrect expectations

Conventional wisdom tells us that we should eat three square meals per day, including a good breakfast, a hearty lunch and filling dinner, and indeed many medical professionals would echo this, with the following statement appearing in the *Journal of Family Healthcare*,[19] a scientific journal commonly read by family physicians and health visitors, 'Parents need to be encouraged to establish a routine of three meals and two snacks a day and not to allow the toddler to set the rules for eating.' How true is this really though and what effect might our dictation of our toddler's eating and overriding of their appetite have upon them in the future?

There is a mounting body of scientific evidence that shows us how parents feed their toddlers can have a lasting effect on their child's eating habits for the rest of their lives. Indeed researcher Leann Birch,[20] who studied food acceptance patterns in the first few years of a child's life at the University of Pennsylvania, says that 'child-feeding practices play a causal role in the development of individual difference in the controls of food intake'. She then goes on to say, 'An enormous amount of learning about food and eating occurs during the transition from the exclusive milk diet of infancy to the omnivore's diet consumed by early childhood. This early learning is constrained by children's genetic predispositions, which include the unlearnt preference for sweet tastes, salty tastes, and the rejection of sour and bitter tastes.' These genetic dispositions are something I will discuss later in this chapter, as it is important that parents understand how toddlers may experience taste very differently to adults.

Birch goes on to say, 'Evidence suggests that children can respond to the energy density of the diet and that although intake at individual meals is erratic, twenty-four-hour energy intake is relatively well regulated. There are individual differences in the regulation of energy intake as early as the preschool period. These individual differences in self-regulation are associated with differences in child-feeding practices.' This should be of great comfort to parents of toddlers, the knowledge that science confirms that while a toddler's food intake may appear sporadic over the course of the day, and is almost certainly not in line with our expectations of three good meals per day, over the course of twenty-four hours it does appear that most toddlers will eat what they need. Birch finishes by saying, 'Initial evidence indicates that imposition of stringent parental controls can potentiate preferences for high-fat, energy-dense foods, limit children's acceptance of a variety of foods, and disrupt children's regulation of energy intake by altering children's responsiveness to internal cues of hunger and satiety. This can occur when well-intended but concerned parents assume that children need help in determining what, when, and how much to eat and when parents impose child-feeding practices that provide children with few opportunities for self-control.'

To sum up: when we try to control our toddler's food intake research suggests that we can cause them to favour unhealthy, fatty food and become out of touch with their own appetite signals. This means that how we handle our toddler's eating habits can and does impact on their eating behaviours for the rest of their lives. The more we control their eating the more out of touch they become with their own hunger and fullness cues and the more likely they are to have eating problems, usually obesity, later in life. That is a shocking thought. It is worth examining in further detail why our actions can have such lasting effects on our toddler's eating habits.

The concept of intuitive eating

Children are born with the innate ability to know how much food their body needs. Instinctively, babies cry when they are hungry and when their stomachs are full they usually drift off to sleep satiated, or push away from the breast or bottle. Recent research[21] shows us that babies weaned by the 'baby led weaning' method 'learn to regulate their food intake in a manner which leads to a lower BMI and a preference for healthy foods like carbohydrates'. In other words babies who are given the freedom to choose what they eat, how they eat it, when they eat it and how much they eat grow up with much better food regulation and a lowered risk of weight problems in later life than those who are weaned to a parent's or 'baby expert's' schedule. Why do we not afford toddlers the same privilege? I am always quite confused when I meet a parent who has weaned their child as a baby following baby led weaning principles and yet now they have a toddler they are highly controlling over their toddler's food intake. Why the difference between babies and toddlers?

Toddlers naturally like to graze constantly and eat small amounts of food and they eat these small amounts of food frequently. The amount and frequency of what they eat is decided by their own innate hunger cues, or what we call their appetite, and when they are hungry they will seek out food, then they will keep eating until they feel full and when they are full they will stop. It's pretty simple really and a pattern we could certainly do with following as adults. During growth spurts, or on particularly busy days, toddlers may seem to be hungry all of the time and on other days, perhaps when they are not so active, or feeling a little under the weather, they have less interest in food. This is the normal way of eating for our species, and what we fail to realise is, as adults, only a tiny minority of us eat 'normally'. We ignore our hunger signals, we eat when we are not hungry, we eat to the clock, we eat socially, we diet, we eat what is expected of us, we eat for comfort, for pleasure, we finish up all of the food on our plates so that it does not go to waste. We do not eat instinctively, well most of us anyway, yet our toddlers do. It is easy to spot what the real problem is.

What parents often don't realise is that their best intentions to keep their toddlers healthy and well nourished often destroy their child's instinctive eating skills. As parents we often believe it is our duty to ensure our child 'eats up all their food', so we bribe them with stickers and dessert and we chastise them for 'not eating up'. Yet what are we really teaching them with these practices? Are we instilling good eating habits into them for life? No, instead we are teaching them to ignore their own innate hunger cues, to override them and to ignore them, which can have lasting consequences for their future eating habits. In our society we teach our children at an early age that food is something they can use to get rewards, food is something to be given to cope with emotions, food is something we give toddlers to keep them quiet or busy, therefore food becomes something that they can then use to fill boredom or an emotional need later in life. Very often too food is something that can become a very stressful, even fearful experience for many toddlers.

As parents we play games to try to encourage our children to eat, we pretend the loaded spoons we are holding are aeroplanes flying into our toddlers' mouths, we praise them, encouraging them to eat more 'Just two more carrots, darling, then you can have some chocolate buttons', we say 'Good boy! You ate it all up!' and our children come home from day care and preschool covered in stickers declaring they were 'good today because I ate up all of my lunch'. What are we really teaching our toddlers with this bizarre behaviour? What we are teaching them is that eating makes mummy and daddy happy, eating is a way to please people, eating is something that brings rewards, eating is a chore. Are these really good beliefs to instil into our toddlers for later in life?

While I agree that it is really important we meet our toddler's basic nutritional needs, I would also argue that we must realise what a lasting effect our actions and words can have. It is imperative that we teach our toddlers that the primary role of food is nourishment, not emotional gain, whether that is for themselves or others. 'Food is fuel' is a good motto to live by. If we can remove the emotional ties with food that most of us, as adults, possess and help our toddler to view food in a much more neutral and healthy way, we can give our children one of the biggest gifts in life, which is a normal relationship with food and in an era of eating disorders and a rising obesity crisis this is a precious gift indeed.

Picky eating as a sign of a need for more control

Consider the following question: why might picky eating behaviour be a sign of a toddler trying to assert more control over their life?

Who decides what our toddlers eat, when they eat it, how they eat it, where they eat it and how much they eat? What about the rest of your toddler's life? What control do they have over when they sleep, when they play, where they go, who they see? We will discuss the idea of control in much more detail in chapter 6. For now I'd like you to consider the following scenario, as the easiest way to answer this is to imagine what it would be like to be a toddler, to put yourself in their place.

Imagine waking at 6am ravenously hungry, yet when you go to ask for breakfast you are told, 'Go back to bed, it's not time to get up yet'. This is only the start though; you reluctantly lie back down in bed with your tummy growling with hunger. Finally, an hour later you are told now it is time to get up, you are led downstairs and served a bowl of warm porridge. You don't really like bitter-tasting porridge; you'd far sooner have a bowl of cornflakes with sugar, but you're told 'don't be silly, porridge is lovely'. You are so hungry you reluctantly eat two-thirds of the bowl of porridge, but then the person who served it to you declares that that isn't good enough, you must eat it all as you need 'a good breakfast inside of you ready for the day ahead'.

You still don't eat so they pick up the spoon, load it with the horrid, bitter-tasting food and ram it into your mouth. That time you were caught unawares; goodness they almost made you gag and vomiting really scares you. It won't happen again though, as next time you're going to keep your mouth firmly closed. They come at you again, notice your gritted teeth and start speaking in a silly baby voice encouraging you to 'open up'; you're not falling for it though so you keep your teeth gritted. Now the baby voice has turned into funny whirring noise and the spoon is flying around your head; apparently it's a helicopter coming into land and the landing pad is in your mouth. Hmm, this isn't fair, you love helicopters and the thought of being a landing pad is a fun one so you open up, oh no, you shouldn't have done, they've put more of the yucky bitter stuff they call 'yummy porridge' in your mouth.

It's 11am now, the trauma of breakfast is over and you're ready for more food, only to be told 'it's not lunchtime yet, darling'. What is this 'lunchtime' that they speak of? Your tummy is ready for food NOW. You are told to 'wait just one more hour', but you don't know what an hour is, you think it might have something to do with the funny bracelet that adults wear on their arms, but you're not sure, so you ask again, perhaps 'an hour' has passed by now. No, apparently it has 'only been five minutes since you last asked'.

Again you don't know what five minutes is; is it longer or shorter than an hour? You don't know but you must eat NOW, so you sneak into the kitchen and raid the cupboard, you've found some bread, it doesn't have any butter on but you don't care, it is just so good to eat, only uh oh, you're in trouble, apparently you shouldn't have done that, you're being screamed at now, 'I said NO, I told you it is not lunchtime yet'.

Finally the mythical 'lunchtime' arrives and you would love some tomato soup, but apparently lunch today is a cheese sandwich. 'That's OK' you think, 'just so long as it's cut into triangles and on my blue plate', only it isn't, it's in squares and it's on a pink plate, you hate pink and you hate squares and even worse it's not the nice yellow cheese, it's the orange cheese that has a funny strong taste that you don't really like. You eat the cucumber wedges you've been given with it instead and beg for more cucumber to fill the hole in your tummy, but you're told you can't have any more 'until you eat your sandwich'. As you're so hungry you have no choice, so you reluctantly eat the cheese that makes your tongue zingy and are delighted when you are told that 'as you've been so good you can have yoghurt'. Apparently you make too much mess when you feed yourself so the yoghurt is fed to you from a spoon; you hate not being able to feed yourself and worse than that you hate someone else putting a spoon into your mouth, it reminds you of when they do 'tooth brushing' every night. You hate tooth brushing, it makes you gag, and being fed this yoghurt reminds you of that, so you start to cry, but now you're being told 'don't be silly you love yoghurt – open wide'. All this and you're still only halfway through the day.

Biological differences in toddler eating

Food neophobia, the fear of trying new foods, is very common in toddlers, particularly towards the second year of life. As parents it is important to understand that a toddler's reluctance to try new foods is usually totally normal. Sometimes reluctance to try new food can be influenced by different things including weaning, how your toddler was fed as a baby and any negative food related events that may have happened, such as choking, which may have conditioned a fear of food in them. In many cases[22] food neophobia can also once again be traced back to parental influences.

Research indicates that exclusively breastfeeding and not introducing solids until the baby is six months old significantly reduces the incidence of food neophobia, a finding that flies in the face of many baby weaning and child cookery experts who say that it is important not to miss the window of opportunity for introducing your baby to new foods. These ideas appear to be based on personal opinion only, rather than scientific evidence. Indeed, recent research found that 'Children who were introduced to complementary foods before 6 months of age had 2.5 times higher odds of developing food neophobia and limited variety of foods... Breastfeeding and introduction of complementary foods after 6 months of age reduced the odds of picky eating during early childhood.'

Why food tastes different to toddlers

Our senses of taste and smell change as we get older. The average adult has approximately 10,000 taste buds, which are located around the tongue, soft palate, the upper portion of the oesophagus and epiglottis. Children have many more taste buds, including some dotted along the insides of their cheeks, which adults do not have. As we age adults' sense of taste remains at roughly the same level, although damage to our taste buds has a dulling effect on them. Our taste buds can be damaged through a variety of events such as smoking or drinking very hot drinks repeatedly, vigorous tongue brushing or scraping and even viral infections.

Research[23] has also indicated that individual variations in the presence of a taste receptor gene influences taste sensitivity in children. This finding may go some way to accounting for our individual differences in taste preferences and food selection. In addition to this age seems to have an effect on the perception of bitterness, with a decline in sensitivity over the years. Children with a certain taste receptor genotype are more sensitive to bitter tastes than adults of the same type; 45 per cent more children than adults were able to detect a bitter taste in an experimental solution used in the research. The lead researcher, developmental psycho-biologist Dr Julie Mennella, commented on the findings of the study saying that 'The sense of taste is an important determinant of what children eat. We know that young children eat what they like. We also know that many children do not like bitter taste, thereby interfering with vegetable consumption and potentially limiting intake of important nutrients.' Dr Mennella then went on to theorise as to how the findings of this and future research could be used to guide us in the future when it comes to toddler eating: 'This type of information will one day help to improve the diets of our children by allowing us to devise better strategies to enhance fruit and vegetable acceptance in children who are sensitive to bitter taste.' Certainly Mennella's research helps us to understand our toddler's reluctance to eat vegetables, particularly those of the green variety: 'It may be that childhood represents a time of heightened bitter taste sensitivity in some children, which lessens with age. Such a scenario would account for the increase of vegetable consumption that often occurs as children mature into adulthood.'

The other point raised in this research that I find most intriguing is that some parents and their children may live in different sensory worlds when it comes to taste, due to differences of taste sensitivity related to our genes, age, or both. Just because we think a certain food is pleasant and tasty it doesn't mean that it tastes appealing to our offspring, Another of the researchers involved in the study commented that 'This knowledge may bring relief to parents who learn that their children reject foods that they themselves like because of inborn differences in taste ability, rather than rebelliousness or defiance of authority.'

With all this new information in mind we learn that, most likely, it is us as parents who really have a problem with our toddler's eating behaviour. It is likely that our toddlers are behaving perfectly normally with their dislike of an adult eating routine, or the foods that we choose to feed them, most likely because of biological differences and also possibly some psychological effects. I have found this information very reassuring, as my youngest child, at five years old, is not keen on her food and I often comment to my husband that she eats like a sparrow. I have long since accepted that this is just the way she is and that her eating habits are normal and as somebody who has rather less than normal eating habits after years of non-instinctive eating, encouraged by my parents through the same loving concern that led me to try to control my firstborn's eating, I am only too pleased to celebrate these. I know if I respect her natural eating patterns and appetite she is likely to grow into an adult with a healthy relationship with food. I am just surprised that, given the growing obesity crisis in the Western world, govern-ments do not encourage the promotion of instinctive or normal eating, rather than perpetuating the myths of portion control, the importance of three meals per day and minimising snacks and, perhaps the biggest lie of all, the effectiveness of diets.

Suggestions for easier toddler eating

Here are my suggestions for easier toddler eating. Try them with your child. Some tips will suit them and some may not, and I'm sure you will come up with variations of your own, in light of the above.

- Respect your child's natural appetite. If they say they are not hungry then respect their decision. If they want more food than you think they should have, listen to them and respect that too.

- Respect that your child may not always be hungry to the clock, for instance at 8am, noon and 5pm when you would usually eat. It is not unheard of for toddlers to want to eat every hour until 3pm and then eat nothing more until the next day. Remember it is our time based eating routine that can be seen as abnormal.

- Respect that your toddler may have different taste preferences to you. Just because you find a food delicious it doesn't mean that it is delicious to your toddler.

- Give your toddler some control over what they eat; let them make choices as much as possible.

- Let your toddler be involved in the preparation of their own food wherever possible. In my family we take this tip the extra mile and my children also get involved in growing their own food. Each spring they select a packet of seeds in the local garden centre and plant them in our vegetable garden, they then tend to them throughout the growing season before harvesting them, and take great pride in eating the food they have grown themselves. We also have an annual family 'potato planting day' in the spring and much fun ensues in the summer when they climb into the vegetable patch, always bare-footed, to play 'hunt the potatoes'. In the summer they also have their own soft fruit patch full of strawberries, raspberries, blackberries and blueberries that they are free to graze on while playing in the garden.

- Let your toddler feed themselves wherever possible. This means ditching the aeroplane and train spoonfuls of food chugging or soaring into their mouths. Yes it is terribly messy, as you'll know if you used baby led weaning, but it is such a different sensory experience for toddlers if they feed themselves and crucially it gives them that all-important control.

- Present food in fun ways: you could use colourful plates; use biscuit cutters to make sandwiches into fun shapes, make vegetable dinosaurs or fruit hedgehogs.

- Make mealtimes an enjoyable social occasion. Toddlers are more likely to eat in emotionally positive atmospheres, so it is vital that you stay calm yourself. If you are positive and relaxed at mealtimes your child is far more likely to be relaxed, which is more likely to have a positive effect on their eating.

- Sit at a table together. Older siblings and parents act as role models to encourage the tasting of novel foods.

- Keep offering foods that are disliked. Repeated exposure to initially disliked foods can help, but don't force the toddler to eat it; if they choose to leave the broccoli on the side of their plate untouched for the fifteenth time that's just fine, and it might take them another three years before they take a bite, but it is important to let them make that choice.

- If you are out and about pack up a small graze box to take with you so that your toddler does not get too hungry waiting for food or having to struggle with food neophobia at a restaurant.

- Consider having a carpet picnic. Have you ever noticed how much children love picnics? There is no reason why picnics should only occur outside in the warm weather. Carpet picnics, with food served buffet style, are always winners with small children.

Sarah's and Gemma's stories below highlight the use of several of these tips, as they discuss how they tackled their own children's picky eating.

Sarah's story

My daughter is a grazer; she always has been. When she started eating solids she was not overly enthusiastic, preferring to continue to breastfeed as much as possible, little and often. She's almost ten now and baby led weaning was not really out there in the public domain at the time we started on the weaning journey or that would definitely have been the path we'd have gone down. She barely touched purees but quickly showed more enthusiasm for finger foods as she got a little older.

As she headed into toddlerhood, I was frequently encountering pressure from family members to get her to finish what she was given to eat and for me to give her more so she ate three meals like adults. I have always been very determined that she shouldn't be forced, cajoled or otherwise coerced into eating everything on her plate but retain the ability to recognise her body's 'full-up' signals and act on them. One of the most influential things I read when she was this age was something that said it is the parent's responsibility to offer the child nutritious food and the child's responsibility to eat it. So I did the planning and the thinking and making sure that over a period of time her food intake was reasonably balanced. Then I tried really hard (and it is hard; we invest so much emotion in food) to let her get on with it, although obviously staying with her while she ate.

My leaving her autonomy over how much she ate combined with a natural (for most toddlers) disinclination to sit still for more than a few minutes meant grazing plates worked really well. I think, also, she got bored with too much of the same thing so small portions of lots of different things kept her interest in her food, even with the whole of the newly accessible world to explore.

We continued to use this method in packed lunches when she needed them at preschool because she was never overly keen on sandwiches. Some people I know use 'monkey plates', which are divided into different sections but we never bought anything special, except a stack of tiny plastic containers. Things I have put in them, or on plates for grazing, include pieces of cucumber, cherry tomatoes, olives, slices of pepper and carrot, fingers of pitta bread, crackers, bread sticks, slices of cooked meat (back in her younger days when she ate meat), cheese, cocktail sausages, Quorn mini-eggs, tofu. One thing I didn't tend to leave around for free access was fruit because she had horrible problems with weak enamel on her milk teeth and we were advised by the dental consultant to give fruit once a day only.

Gemma's story

When I first started to wean Corey (around six months) he wasn't particularly interested. I tried baby led weaning but he didn't seem ready to pick up the food and experiment; he just wasn't interested. Due to his very broken sleep I felt under pressure to feed him so started to make purees – anything to get some food into him and perhaps stop him waking up so many times per night (four to six times every night without fail). This didn't help and within no time he refused any type of pureed food; he wouldn't even open his mouth.

As he grew older the foods in general that he would try were always very limited; he was happy to eat fruit, yoghurt and anything bread-related but anything that you would call a 'meal' (i.e. spaghetti bolognaise) he refused. I longed to make one dinner for us all but he would never try anything from our plates.

I put this down to a phase and thought that when he grew older he would become more interested, but nothing changed. As time went on I became frustrated that he wasn't eating healthily enough or getting the right nutrients – the lack of vegetables in particular bothered me. Compared to friends' children of similar ages, his eating habits were poor and, as usual, I wondered what I could be doing wrong, or what poor relationships with food we may have set up.

I tried different ways of cooking the food, offering something he liked with something new on his plate each time, sitting at the table together as a family so he could see us eating too, using particular bowls/plates/cutlery. Even cutting food into fun shapes had no effect whatsoever. It became clear over time that nothing was going to change and no matter what different tactics I tried, he was very strong-willed and if he didn't want to eat something, there was no way it was going to pass his lips.

Then I came across an article about toddlers and eating and realised that Corey is a grazer and that it's typical toddler behaviour to snack throughout the day rather than eat meals at set times. So I started to follow his lead and allow him to eat when he wanted to; I realised he was so busy playing a lot of the time and what he wanted was to play and then eat something, play some more and come back later . . . and so on. I had to relax any ideas I had about us sitting at the table eating meals together (just as I'd seen friends doing); it just wasn't going to work for us and I became quickly aware that if I forced him into doing this I may end up creating issues around food for him.

Now at two and a half he is very much the same; he is wary of many foods and won't try them, but there are many that he likes too and we just work with those ones instead. I still try to introduce new things, mostly to no avail, but perhaps in time he might try them. He still grazes throughout the day and in a lot of ways I actually prefer the flexibility and relaxed nature of this way of eating; I am in fact a bit of a grazer myself. That's not to say though that he won't sit at the table at a restaurant and enjoy a family meal – in fact he loves eating out. Most of all I am happy that we have followed his lead and allowed him to read his body and decide what he needs.

Chapter 5

Carrots and sticks and the problem with praise

What we instil in our children will be the foundation upon which they build their future.

Dr Steve Maraboli, author and philanthropist

Most parents know about common behaviourist methods of discipline such as sending your child to 'time out' and making them sit on the 'naughty step' when they have done something unacceptable. You probably also know about methods to reinforce so called 'good behaviour', such as reward charts, adding marbles to a jar with the promise of a special treat when the jar is full and piling on the praise when your child has done something that you are happy about. In my world these methods are called 'carrots and sticks'. The former are the proverbial 'dangled carrots' or rewards designed to elicit repetition of the desired behaviour and the latter are the 'beating sticks', a form of punishment (although no longer physical) hopefully to result in extinction of the undesirable behaviour. These are the methods we see used in parenting programmes on television, are advocated by health professionals, widely employed in the education system and are probably used by most of your friends and family, for they are very commonly recommended.

What if I told you that I didn't believe any of these methods worked? Not in the long term anyway. What if I told you I thought they carried significant risks and side effects, including something as seemingly innocuous as praise? Would that surprise you? What if I told you I believed that these methods are actually all forms of punishment, even the carrots?

I imagine this may come as quite a shock. Especially given that almost everything in mainstream society tells you this is 'the way' to raise children. When I researched this after having my first two children and using most of the above methods I felt absolutely floored. Exactly what **was** I meant to do instead then? Had I caused my children some sort of irreparable harm by using carrots and sticks? The confusion and guilt was immense, but thankfully short lasting. Although I now believe in an entirely different way of parenting I know that I was doing my best at the time, with what resources I had available to me, and in many ways I feel privileged that I had discovered a different way, for some parents never do. I took steps to resolve some of the issues that had resulted from the techniques I had used too, and this is something we will discuss in chapter 12.

The case against punishments

So, what exactly is the problem with the use of carrots and sticks? First, let us consider the sticks; the use of punishments to control behaviour. Here I would like to focus on the most common toddler punishments, such as 'time out', 'naughty steps' (or corners), consequences (such as losing a treat or favourite toy) or simply ignoring the undesirable behaviour. This quote from parenting author Laura Davis sums it up well for me:

> Behind every behaviour is an impulse or an attempt to communicate that can be supported. Even 'hostile' gestures can come from a basic desire to communicate. People hurt others only as much as they themselves are hurting. When they hurt others it is because they are often feeling hurt, mad or scared themselves. A child who pushes another child out of the toy car may be feeling crowded and scared. When a child is hurting other children it may be hard to remember that he's feeling vulnerable or scared himself. But if you merely punish him you load more hurt onto the existing hurt. If instead you take into account his circumstances and motivation, you can approach conflict resolution from a less punitive perspective than 'let's punish the wrongdoer'.

I wonder why we focus on punishing our toddlers for **giving** us a hard time, when in fact it is toddlers that need our support for they are **having** a hard time. Would we still punish them if we realised and acknowledged the trauma they were feeling?

We know from previous chapters that many things toddlers do, that we consider 'naughty', are merely a reflection of their immature brain development. How might they feel if we punish them for something that they cannot control or, more than that, punish them for a behaviour that is really only exhibiting their big feelings and confusion, a cry for help you might say. Remember the bungalow metaphor and the billowing smoke of big uncomfortable feelings uncontrollably exploding out of the chimney? Such an uncontrolled explosion must surely be scary to endure.

What if it were you?

Consider the following scenario:

> Imagine that you wake up one morning with a nasty virus and find that you have lost your voice. You try all manner of remedies and medicines but nothing works, nothing brings back your voice. The virus hasn't just affected your vocal cords though; it's caused problems with your fine motor control too, particularly, that in your hands and fingers, you find it almost impossible to form a pincer grip and as a result you cannot hold a pen to write your words down. You can't talk and you can't write; however will you communicate?
>
> At first it's not so bad. You can still nod and shake your head, and you can still point. Your family are patient with you; they feel really sad for you and sympathise with your illness, fetching you chicken soup, hot water bottles and blankets. Three days go past. You begin to feel better; you have much more energy, but your voice is still lost and your muscles still ache, making it impossible to write. Patience has worn thin among your family now; they are getting irritated with running around after you and you in turn are getting increasingly irritated with your lack of ability to communicate and make yourself understood by your nearest and dearest.
>
> You really want pasta for lunch with a glass of fresh orange juice to drink, but your partner has made you a cheese sandwich with a cup of tea. You are still feeling a little tender in the head and would really like some peace and quiet, but your son has his stereo on really loudly. You would love to read a magazine, but when you look for it you find somebody has moved it and you can't find it. You are feeling a little chilly and would love somebody to light

a fire, but wait a minute; your daughter is opening the window, making you even colder. You go off to search out your favourite blanket to snuggle on the sofa, but it's in the washing machine. Who did that? Didn't they know it was your favourite blanket and you needed it now to soothe yourself? You look at the blanket helplessly, spinning around and around inside the washing machine and you involuntarily stamp your foot. Out of sheer exhausting frustration you decide to have a nap, but just as you lay your head down and close your eyes your partner decides now is a good moment to take you out to the shops, and as they drag you by your hand and tell you to put your coat on they say 'fresh air will do you good'. You hesitate so they grip your hand a little tighter, encouraging you out of the door. They bribe you with the idea of cake at the local coffee shop as a treat 'if you're good and put your coat on like I've told you to'.

All you want to do though is curl up with your favourite blanket, a bowl of pasta and a glass of orange juice and your magazine in peace and quiet, and then to have a little sleep. You feel so powerless, like you aren't in control of your own life any more. If only you could tell your family how you were feeling. If only you could get the words out, if only you could write them down, if only you could just make them understand. The frustration is overwhelming; you've never felt anything like it. You begin to experience the feelings of helplessness, sadness and frustration giving way to something else; a feeling of anger bubbles up in your tummy in a burning rage and at the same time fat, heavy tears begin to roll down your cheek. It's all too much; you just can't cope any more and you can't control your emotions, which is only exacerbated by how tired and hungry you now feel (since you didn't eat the cheese sandwich your partner made for you because you really wanted pasta).

All of a sudden you flip. You pick up a vase on the table next to you and throw it to the other side of the room in frustration ... as it shatters in tiny pieces you feel the tiniest bit of release as you break down in sobs, hitting the floor repeatedly with your fist, but now that release has turned to fear, fear that you can't control your feelings and your emotions, fear that you will never be calm again. You really need somebody now, more than ever, to hold you, to tell you it will be OK, to help you to calm down and control these big, out-of-control feelings.

Imagine yourself in the scenario above. How would you hope your family would respond? You would like them to respond with a warm hug and gentle words telling you 'I'm here, we'll be OK, and I'll help you to calm down'. I imagine you would hope and expect your family to respond to you with understanding and compassion.

Imagine then how you would feel if instead of the calm, gentle and soothing response you so desperately need, they harshly dragged you to a corner of the room instead, told you that you had 'been naughty' and that you had to sit on a small plastic step, facing the wall, for five minutes and that if you moved your time would start over again. This is your punishment for 'being naughty' for smashing the vase and 'throwing a tantrum' when you hit your hands on the floor and screamed 'in a baby voice'.

Your partner tells you they hope you have learnt from this experience, that next time you 'mustn't be naughty'. You feel embarrassed, ashamed, misunderstood, frustrated, sad, angry and unloved. What did you do wrong? You were only trying to communicate, to ask them for help, in the only way you could; the world is just so overwhelming now you can't communicate properly and you have all of these big, new, scary emotions that you can't handle by yourself.

I know that scenario seems incredibly far-fetched; of course we would never treat an adult like that, and come to think of it surely we wouldn't treat any human being like that? What about toddlers though? How often do we ignore what their behaviour is trying to communicate to us, how often do we control their day? How often do we show them it's OK to have these big feelings, recognising that a tantrum is just as scary to a toddler as it is annoying and sometimes scary to you too? How often do we afford toddlers the same level of compassion as we do adults? These may be disturbing thoughts, but I often wonder why we can't see how we are treating our toddlers and how at odds our treatment of them is when compared to our long-term goals and aspirations for them.

I love this quote from psychologist Dr Alice Miller, 'We don't yet know, above all, what the world might be like if children were to grow up without being subjected to humiliation, if parents would respect them and take them seriously as people.' What if we respected our toddlers? What difference would that make in our lives, in theirs and to future generations of our family? I don't think it is too crazy to wonder what would happen to the world and the future of humanity as a whole if we were all treated with compassion and respect from day one, since what we do as parents has enormous potential and long lasting consequences.

Punishing or ignoring (for ignoring a toddler's big feelings is still a punishment) a toddler does nothing to encourage them to behave in a more sociable way; remember that they are not yet capable of the rational and analytical thoughts that adults have. Toddlers do not sit on a naughty step and contemplate what they have done; they simply can't, their under-developed neocortex does not allow them that privilege. At best a toddler will sit, or perhaps stand, in time out and learn to disguise their feelings, they might learn that it may be better for them to conserve their energy and bring the scary big feelings inwards, to shut down their externally conveyed emotions as it were, but it doesn't mean they are not experiencing inner turmoil. This is illustrated in a quote from Jane Nelsen, author of *Positive Discipline*, 'Where did we ever get the crazy idea that in order to make children do better, first we have to make them feel worse? Think of the last time you felt humiliated or treated unfairly. Did you feel like cooperating or doing better?'

Make no mistake, when a toddler quietens on the naughty step, by no means does this mean that they are no longer feeling the big feelings; their cortisol (stress hormone) levels will still be high, their body will be tense with anxiety, they will just show no outward symptoms. This is a state termed as 'learned help-lessness' by psychologist Martin Seligman.

Fighting for attention

I have long been confused by the assertion from some toddler experts, who subscribe to the behaviourist view of child rearing, that toddlers only behave in a certain way, particularly when they tantrum, in order for us to give them our attention. With this in mind they commonly suggest you should 'ignore the bad behaviour' and instead 'pile on the praise when he's good'. This method firstly completely ignores the toddler's needs, perhaps at a time when they need you the most, for there is always a reason why a toddler needs your attention, and secondly shows that your attention and thereby your love is conditional.

As author of the book *Playful Parenting*, Dr Lawrence Cohen so eloquently sums it up: 'I'm always amazed when adults say that children "just did that to get attention". Naturally children who need attention will do all kinds of things to get it. Why not just give it to them?' Love withdrawal techniques, such as time out or ignoring a child also makes our love conditional, teaching the child that we only love them when they are 'good'. In many cases this can compound the issue at hand, making the toddler feel worse and perhaps almost guaranteeing that they will 'misbehave' even more in order to get the attention they so crave in the future. This is particularly true when the child's unwanted behaviour is initially sparked by a need for more love and attention, for instance the arrival of a new sibling, an unsettling life change that the majority of toddlers are forced to negotiate.

Psychologist Martin Hoffman believes that time out is crueller than any other punishment, as the child has no understanding of why he has been bad and similarly no knowledge of when the parent is coming back. This heightened loss of parental love does work at controlling behaviour, but at terrific cost. Indeed the very idea of 'time out' came from the process of 'time out from positive reinforcement', an exercise initially used to suppress behaviour in laboratory rats, for instance with sensory deprivation or removal of food in order to control behaviour. Sadly, as with much of behaviourism, these unethical animal-based experiments grew into what is now the leading approach to child discipline. A scary thought indeed. The shutting down of external emotional display does not reflect the fact the toddler has made a considered decision to 'calm down and be good'; rather it shows a toddler who endures these punishments and has been trained to be quiet through a simple process of classical conditioning, which is the very same, century old, behavioural principle on which the laboratory rats were trained. Everything in life has risks and the risks with this type of behavioural control are big. If a parent chooses to use these punishments I firmly believe they should be made aware of the risks.

Perhaps, rather than treating our toddlers in the same way lab rats are treated we might consider the answer instead to be for us to provide unconditional love and a safe environment for the child to express their unwanted feelings. I will explore this idea in much more detail in chapter 12 when we discuss the concept of responding to our toddlers with compassion.

Time out the ToddlerCalm™ way

The only 'time out' I advocate is the use of 'time out for parents', where instead of removing the toddler, at times of high stress the parent may decide to retreat, whether physically or mentally, for a few short moments, in order to calm themselves down so they may respond appropriately and respectfully to their child. There is a longer version of this too; some people call it 'me time', taking time to nurture your own needs so that you may parent with patience and compassion. If you are exhausted or 'full up' with stress and tension it will be almost impossible for you to take on board your child's big emotions, and taking care of your own needs then is perhaps the most important thing you can do as a parent, but so often so many parents neglect themselves and their children suffer as a result. Parenting a toddler is really draining, both physically and emotionally, and it is therefore vital that you take time out to relax and recuperate yourself. This is such an important concept we will look at it in much more depth in chapter 12.

The case against rewards

So, if punishments are not the way to go, what about rewards? Surely all toddlers like to receive rewards, whether they are stickers, chocolate, a trip to the park or parental attention? Surely a few little stickers carry no harm? After all everybody tells you to 'ignore the bad behaviour and reward the good'. This process is entrenched in society and continues all the way through the education system. My children still come home from school every day covered in stickers and clutching merit certificates for their 'good behaviour'; they even get awards merely for just attending school.

Rewards do carry risks; in some ways they can be even more detrimental than punishments and although they may seem to work, in the long term they most certainly do not, in fact they may cause more future problems than if you had never used them at all.

Here is an example of this, from my own family.

What will you give me if I do it?

'What will you give me if I do it?'

I had just asked my son, then nine, if he could help me to set the table for dinner.

'Can I have £2 if I do it?' he asked.

Today it was £2, tomorrow perhaps £3, and what would it be in ten years' time? Yesterday (well seven years previously actually) it was a sticker on his Thomas the Tank Engine reward chart. This was something that seemed like such a good idea at the time. A way to encourage him to tidy up, brush his teeth and eat his vegetables, and never did I anticipate the long lasting, undesirable, effects it would have.

What do we teach our children when we aim to modify their behaviour by rewarding them with stickers on a chart, marbles in a jar or promising 'if you do that, then I'll do this'? Apparently I had taught my child that helping people was only worth doing if you are given a reward for doing so.

When you have a tantruming two-year-old, whose favourite word is 'no' (usually uttered over and over again) and who falls screaming to the floor in the supermarket at the drop of a hat (or taking away of a chocolate bar they have pilfered from the shelf and decided that they absolutely must have, now), refuses to brush his teeth, wakes at 5am every single day and prefers to poo in his pants than in his potty, rewards, or – as I prefer to call them – bribery, are a very tempting way to get a toddler to do what you want. Reward charts are behaviourism at its simplest and most effective; it is dog training for toddlers. Indeed behavioural control is a doddle if you dangle carrots in front of your toddler, but, and it's a big 'but', what we don't necessarily realise when choosing these methods is why they work and why these reasons are so vitally important to the relationship and behaviour you are creating in your child for years to come.

Why do reward charts, and any other manner of carrot dangling, seem to work? Let me introduce you to the concept of extrinsic (external) versus intrinsic (internal) motivation. Rewards, such as sticker charts, 'if then' promising ('**if** you let little Johnny share your toy **then** I'll buy you a new book'), marbles in a jar and so on, work on increasing extrinsic motivation. Increasing extrinsic motivation means using an external motivator (in this example a book), which works by encouraging your child to behave in a certain way in order to receive said reward. This is a classic behavioural tool, classical conditioning at its best. Examples may include 'eat all your dinner and you can have a chocolate', 'brush your teeth and you can have a sticker', 'if you pick up your toys then we'll go to the park' and it works, or does it? I guess it depends on your definition of 'works'. There is no denying that these methods work, but how and for how long?

I love this quote from poet W. H. Auden written in 1970, as it illustrates this point so clearly: 'Of course, behaviourism "works". So does torture. Give me a no-nonsense, down-to-earth behaviourist, a few drugs, and simple electrical appliances, and in six months I will have him reciting the Athanasian Creed in public.'

In the short term rewarding the behaviour you want via the use of stickers, sweets and so on works well and, most importantly for you as a parent, it works quickly. However, as with cutting corners in any other aspect of child rearing you pay a price for that short term gain. The effects of sticker charts and other similar methods of rewards are not long lasting, rather they are incredibly superficial.

For a real change to take place, and by that I mean changing the child's internal drives, leaving them wanting to do, or indeed not do, something for no other reason than **they** want to, we need to work with a child's intrinsic motivation, that is the motivation that comes from within. Rewards such as sticker charts work only on a superficial extrinsic level, which, while they produce quick results for little effort and financial outlay, can actually undermine intrinsic motivation, causing you and your child untold heartache in the future.

A fascinating related example here is the history of blood donation in the USA versus Britain. In Britain blood donors have never received any financial benefit for donating blood, yet in America donors were once paid. Which country do you think donated more blood? Surely you would think the financial incentive in America would result in more citizens giving blood? Think again, it was the unpaid, indeed unrewarded British who donated more. The intrinsic motivation of donating blood merely to help people in need proved more of a motivation than the extrinsic one of financial reward.

What does that mean then? In short, these techniques of behavioural control through rewards make your child **less** likely to do the specific task unless they are given a reward. This brings me back to the conversation with my son. It starts with stickers and chocolate buttons, and then it moves onto harder bargaining, usually involving increasing amounts of cash. What do you end up giving a sixteen-year-old burly teenager to do something? A sticker just won't cut it there, so what do you do? As author of the book *Punished by Rewards*, Alfie Kohn, says, 'the more we want children to want to do something, the more counterproductive it will be to reward them for doing it.'

The sort of motivation provided by stickers and chocolate is not really changing behaviour at all, far from it; it is actually a form of compliance tool. By this I mean that your child is not learning 'right and wrong', nor are they becoming a better person, instead they are complying with their behaviour while the reward is on offer, so remove the reward and you lose compliance. Compliance absolutely does not indicate that an internally motivated change has taken place.

Then there is also the issue of the compliant teenager. As a toddler compliance sure is appealing when you are in the supermarket, desperate to get your shopping and out with the least embarrassment possible; for us as parents in this situation compliance is very appealing. Now imagine your compliant toddler has grown into a teenager and he is in the school playground with his friends. His friends are trying to encourage him to smoke, offering him a cigarette with chants of 'go on, go on', the unspoken assumption being that if he takes it and begins smoking he will be 'cooler' and thus more accepted by his peers. Now, if your teen is used to being compliant, doing something to get a reward (a sticker or peer regard is very little different here) he will be far more likely to comply, to buckle to peer pressure and to start smoking. I bet that wasn't something you thought could ever be related to how you dealt with him at the age of two?

The issue with rewards doesn't just end there though. Science backs up much of what is really common sense with a large amount of research investigating the effects of rewards on the intrinsic motivation of children, yet we don't seem to hear much about this research. From the popularity of rewards as a method of behavioural control you would think that all of science backs up the idea, wouldn't you?

This assumption, however, could not be further from the truth. Just because you might not have heard of the research does not mean it doesn't exist. I've always wondered why it isn't more widely known and realise that I agree with the world-renowned obstetrician Dr Michel Odent, who labels this sort of research that never sees the light of day 'cul-de-sac epidemiology', in other words research that is hidden away with no through access to wider society, just like the end of a road in a cul-de-sac. Why do we hide this research away? I believe we do this with any research that is too uncomfortable for us to deal with as a society, which questions the values we hold and the actions we take, for fear of guilt and unease. I am a keen advocate of making this research as widely known as possible, whether it is relating to birth, babies or, in this case, toddlers.

I have already mentioned the fascinating blood donation statistics in the UK and USA, which provide sound quantitative evidence for the effects rewards have on intrinsic and extrinsic motivation; these results too have been replicated many times in laboratory tests. Take for instance research conducted in Germany in 2008,[24] which studied the influence of giving twenty-month-old toddlers rewards and verbal praise on helping behaviours, finding that those who received a reward or praise were less likely to help in the future than those who were not. As the researchers Warneken and Tomasello summarised in their conclusions, 'This ... effect suggests that even the earliest helping behaviours of young children are intrinsically motivated and that socialization practices involving extrinsic rewards can undermine this tendency.'

Further research[25] looking at slightly older children, aged seven to eleven years, supports the idea that rewards reduce intrinsic motivation in children, particularly when related to altruistic, helping behaviour. In this experiment the children were given the opportunity to sort coloured paper into stacks, and they were told that their efforts would benefit sick children in hospital. Some of the children were told that they would be rewarded for their efforts, while others were not. The children were then given a second opportunity to volunteer their help after the initial experimentation phase. Unsurprisingly the children who were rewarded for the earlier task were significantly less helpful than those who were intrinsically motivated to help, without rewards. The rewarded children spent far less time on the voluntary tasks and completed much less work than those who were unrewarded. The researchers also found that those children who were rewarded regularly at home by their parents were the least helpful of all.

Looking at alternatives to rewards and praise, research in 2006[26] suggested that when it comes to helpful behaviour children are most influenced by their parents' actions and behaviour. If parents model altruistic and empathic behaviour and explain their reasoning to their children then the children are likely to copy them. Many of these behaviours modelled by the adults concerned parenting and how the parents behaved towards their children, for instance by displaying parental warmth, allowing the child to form a secure emotional attachment with them, helping their children to regulate their negative emotions and big feelings and the avoidance of punishments. The very things we don't do when we parent through the use of carrots and sticks.

Perhaps what we really need to encourage in our children is free thought, confidence and trust in the hope that they will grow into an empathic adult by modelling the empathy shown to them as a child. Unfortunately our society is so entrenched in the idea of controlling children that the very idea that the best approach may not be to control them through strict discipline is a shocking one. The thought that our children would perhaps end up as kinder, more altruistic adults if we did not constantly punish wrongdoings and reward good is a difficult thought to entertain, for it is so alien to what society believes. As psychologist Joseph Chilton Pearce says, 'We have a cultural notion that if children were not engineered, if we did not manipulate them, they would grow up as beasts in the field.

This is the wildest fallacy in the world.' For many it is a huge leap of faith to ignore conventional advice that is endorsed by most educational establishments, popular media, parenting experts and many healthcare workers. I hope that the evidence presented in this chapter will help you to have the confidence to ignore these often well-meant, but misguided suggestions in the future.

Are rewards always bad?

I am often asked if I really never use rewards. I am always honest and answer 'no, sometimes I do'. Many parents are concerned that moving away from using rewards is such a big step that sometimes they will unconsciously use them and then be concerned about the damage they have caused to their child. Please don't worry. I believe rewards are not the way to go as a main line of defence, but sometimes, very rarely, I do think that they have a small place, but it is important that you do not rely on them as your main parenting strategy. For example, I work from home, which is usually complete chaos with four loud children. Quite often I will receive an important business telephone call while my children are charging around the house shouting at the top of their lungs, and often they will decide that it is time for a full-on sibling war just as I pick up the telephone to make a call. I have been known then to suggest they are 'rewarded' for being quiet by doing something that could be considered a treat, whether that is making popcorn or spending more time on their games console than I would ordinarily allow. In that moment I need them to be quiet and this is the quickest way of achieving it, so that I may continue with my call in peace. I am mindful to use this technique as sparingly as possible, but do not feel too guilty if that is what I need to resort to from time to time.

Similarly many parents ask me 'but my toddler gets covered in stickers at preschool, is that bad?' or 'my child's school uses reward charts, will that undo everything I'm doing?', and usually my answer is along the lines of what you do with your child at home will have the biggest effect on them, but if you are concerned why not speak to the preschool or school and ask them to consider other methods? If you are not happy with the way your child is being treated do not be afraid to ask the educational setting to use a different strategy.

The problem with praise

It might be time to rethink our usage of punishments and rewards as the main tools in our toddler parenting toolkit, but how about praise? Praise is surely only ever good? Praise could never be harmful? Think again. As psychologist Haim Ginott commented in 1965, 'Praise, like penicillin, must not be administered haphazardly. There are rules and cautions that govern the handling of potent medicines – rules about timing and dosage, cautions about possible allergic reactions. There are similar regulations about the administration of emotional medicine.'

Perhaps the biggest part of the problem is that the majority of praise we give to our small children is very shallow. I am guilty of all of the following, as it is almost impossible to stop them slipping out sometimes; after all most of us were raised on comments such as these:

'Good boy'
'Well done'
'Good job'

Praise like this can actually have the opposite effect of that desired; maybe it might cause your child to lose interest in the task and not push themselves to do better next time, maybe they might feel that you only love them if they 'do good'. Praise can lead children to believe they are only 'good' if they are perfect, which in turn can lead to a fear of failure. When we praise only the good outcomes we forget the effort they put into tying their shoelaces for an hour, before they eventually gave up and had to ask you to help. Would we praise their effort, even though they did not complete the task? Is a child's perseverance and tenacity at a task that they find hard surely not more worthy of praise than that of a normal body function, like a singular wee in a potty, and a time when we usually heap on the praise? Constantly telling a child 'good job' is meaningless and shallow at best; at worst you can lower self-esteem and create a 'praise junkie'. Remember my earlier example of the teenager being encouraged to smoke for the first time by his peers. Maybe, therefore, it is time to change our language and drop the constant shallow praise?

How to use praise effectively

Psychologists Henderlong and Lepper[27] have examined over thirty years' worth of combined studies looking at the effects of praise and have concluded that providing some guidelines are kept in mind then praise can be an effective way of motivating children. Their guidelines include always praising with sincerity and specificity, praising children only on traits that it is possible for them to change, praising using clear, descriptive language, withholding praise for achievements that come easily to children and for things that they already enjoy, praising children for their desire to master skills more than the outcomes, never comparing your child to others in your praise and always being mindful of your child's own individual development. Using these guidelines we can see that there are thankfully ways to use praise effectively that are not going to backfire in the future.

Say what you see

I believe one of the most important and easiest ways to use praise effectively is the 'Say what you see' approach, often termed 'descriptive praise'. In this approach you literally act as a commentator of your child's life. Think of a football commentator or a sports presenter commenting on the Grand Prix. Perhaps you may say things such as 'I see you are building a very long track for your trains and now you are driving them under the bridge' or 'You've used lots of colours in that picture; I can see the colours red, blue and green in the flowers'. By describing what you see you are affirming to your toddler that you are interested in what they are doing and that you are giving them your undivided attention. Toddlers thrive on this form of praise and it is very easy to do once you get used to it.

Ask your toddler questions

The second most common approach to praising your toddler effectively is by questioning them: 'Why did you choose that colour for the house in your picture?' or 'Why did you dress your dolly in that dress today?' This shows your toddler that you are genuinely interested in what they are doing and appreciative of the amount of effort they are putting in. This form of praise is wonderful for eliciting a conversation about what your toddler is doing and often their answers are fascinating.

Model self-praise

Another tactic is to model self-praise: admittedly this does feel more than a little uncomfortable at first, but if your toddler observes you praising yourself for your own effort they are likely to follow suit. For instance, if you have just tackled a particularly large load of washing you may say to yourself, out loud, 'I'm so proud of myself for doing all of this washing. I wasn't sure I had the energy to do it, but I'm happy that I got through it all.' This sort of modelling by you encourages your toddler to take pride in the work that they do; the ultimate intrinsic motivation you might say.

Be clear and specific

Any praise you do give should be as clear and specific as possible; this helps your child to understand exactly what it is they have done that they should be proud of. An example here would be to say 'I'm so pleased you put your coat on this morning without me asking, thank you, that has made my morning so much easier', rather than 'Good girl for getting ready'. In the second example the toddler has no idea what it is that they have done that makes them 'good', nor do they know why this behaviour was something that pleased you. If they do not understand then how can they replicate it?

Don't mix praise with a put-down

You should always try to make sure that your praise isn't mixed with a more negative comment, such as, 'I'm so pleased you put your coat on this morning without me asking, thank you. That has made my morning so much easier than the usual terrible mornings I have when you're being difficult and stubborn about getting ready.' In this example the praise turns from something positive, boosting confidence and pride to no more than a verbal punishment.

Never praise eating

There is also one area where I can never advocate the usage of praise, even if presented in a mindful way as discussed above, and that is anything related to eating. The issue of praising a child on anything related to their eating habits is complex and one that I have already covered in quite some depth in chapter 4.

Since launching ToddlerCalm™ I have met many parents who have decided to parent their toddler without the use of strict punishments or conditional rewards. Many are mindful of their usage of praise too, and one such parent is Emma, whose story is particularly interesting, given her background and training.

Emma's story

Musing about becoming a mother while pregnant with my son, I expected the first year to be the hardest as I didn't have much experience with babies. Toddlerhood, though, would be relatively easy I'd thought, as young children were my business. I am an Early Years teacher. I wouldn't need Supernanny to tell me about time out or sticker charts, as I'd done it all before. So as we entered the phase of terrible twos at around twenty-eight months I began to employ the strategies I had been taught and had used for years. However, I soon discovered that using 'behaviour modification' techniques with my own child was drastically different from using them with children in school. I found myself falling into all the common traps: issuing threats, 'If you do that one more time I'm going to put you on the step,' often not following through. And bribery: 'If you get in the buggy you can have a Smartie.' Not only were these ploys completely useless at **modifying** my son's behaviour, I was making both him and me miserable. 'Mummy, why are you being so mean to me?' he began to ask. A very good question!

My parents were living with us at the time and were also at a loss as to how to deal with my son's behaviour but we all agreed that using shame, guilt, coercion and bribery were not the way. I knew that if I were more consistent with my method I might see results but I also knew I didn't want this approach to work. I loved my wilful, lively and mischievous son the way he was and I sensed continuing along this path was not only damaging our relationship but it was also squashing his spirit. Something was seriously flawed with the system that I had assumed for so long was **the way**.

I began to research parenting books and only found more of the same. Finally after taking advice from newly found like-minded parents I came across Alfie Kohn's book, *Unconditional Parenting*. I read the first three chapters in one sitting and can honestly say I have not threatened, bribed or otherwise attempted to control my son since. Instead I have spent a lot more time talking to him, redirecting him or just accepting that his behaviour has a cause that I have created and, thus, to pick my battles. I try to remember that his tricky behaviour is totally normal for his age and that he does not have the fully developed sense of empathy that we adults do. Knowing this has helped me to readjust my expectations and have more patience. I also try to see each incident as a teaching opportunity instead of a battle of wills. Although I still have a lot to learn about this gentler form of parenting (I know I don't get it right a lot of the time), I feel in my heart it is the right path. I also feel my son is **learning** rather than conforming, a distinction that I never appreciated before, but is certainly the most important lesson that I have learnt since becoming a mother.

Introducing the ToddlerCalm™ CRUCIAL™ toddler parenting strategy

For many parents this new understanding of punishment, rewards and praise is eye-opening and often liberating, yet this very discovery can often also leave parents floundering, wondering what they should do instead. This is the 'light bulb, rug pull moment', where it is both deeply enlightening but also disturbing to learn that everything you know may perhaps not be the way forward for your family.

The remainder of this book will be devoted to explaining the alternatives; we will look at ways that you can build communication with your toddler, understand their behaviour, encourage the behaviour you would like to see and reduce the behaviour you would not. You will be able to formulate an action plan that is individual to your family, by means of working through several examples of common toddler concerns. Lastly, you will learn how to use boundaries and limits to remain an authoritative parent, rather than a permissive one who allows their toddler to run riot.

I always wanted ToddlerCalm™ to be something that empowers parents, something that helps them to become their own experts, and use knowledge that they can apply to any situation that they face with their toddlers. By the end of this book you should be able to think 'I have a plan, I know what to do now', whatever the issue they may be facing at that time.

Enter the ToddlerCalm™ CRUCIAL™ parenting strategy, which lists crucial points for all parents of toddlers to remember. It doesn't end there though; CRUCIAL™ can be applied to almost any age, even into adulthood. CRUCIAL™ is the framework by which I hope parents will be able to generate their own ideas and solutions for parenting their toddler, whatever problem you may have. There are no prescribed ways of dealing with certain situations, as there can be no one size fits all solution for coping with your toddler's behaviour. All toddlers and parents are unique; therefore each solution must be unique too.

Just to remind you, the CRUCIAL™ acronym stands for:

Control
Rhythm
Understanding
Communication
Individual
Avoidance
Love

Throughout the rest of the book I devote a chapter to each of the CRUCIAL™ points and in chapter 14 I work through some examples of CRUCIAL™ in practice to give you a good idea of how each of the points can be applied to different real life examples.

Chapter 6

The battle for CONTROL

*The fundamental condition of childhood
is powerlessness.*

Jane Smiley, novelist

I have often heard people describe toddlers as 'manipulative', 'controlling' and having their parents 'wrapped around their little finger'. In reality I believe nothing could be further from the truth. If we really think about how much control a toddler has, not only over their parents but over every facet of their own life, it is actually minuscule.

How much control do toddlers really have?

Think of an average day for a toddler: they might naturally wake at 6am, but are told that 'It is not morning yet; go back to sleep';

they may not be hungry but are told they 'need to eat breakfast', or perhaps they may fancy something different for breakfast than that which they are given. After breakfast it's time to get dressed: does the toddler choose whether they get dressed or not? Do they choose when they get dressed? Do they choose what they wear? Do they choose who gets them dressed? Usually the answer is 'No'. Many toddlers would probably like to spend all day naked or wearing a Spiderman costume if they had the choice, but we decide that is not acceptable.

My toddlers hated to wear anything made from wool, yet I still bought woollen jumpers to keep them warm; my daughter loved to wear a rainbow of colours, all at once, and it took all of my willpower not to say, 'That doesn't match, you can't wear those together, they look silly.' One of my sons used to love getting himself dressed, but he was painfully slow, so I often took over and hurriedly dressed him. Who is in control in all of these scenarios? The parent or the toddler?

Think about how little control a toddler has even when they've only been up for an hour or two. The day continues, we choose where they go, we choose what and when they eat, we choose their nap time, we choose their bath time, we choose their entertainment, be that arranging a playdate, going to nursery or watching the television. At nursery their day is controlled by others who decide when it is playtime, when it is story time, when it is tidy-up time and when it is snack time. Even during so-called 'free play' the choice is often not really free, but the adult selects a small variety of activities that the toddler may choose from.

Back at home we continue to choose toddlers' toys and we often control their play. We also control the bigger activities in their life too, from deciding when it's time for them to move to a 'big bed', to give up the dummy and bottles or wean from the breast, when it is time for them to potty train and when they are to welcome a younger sibling. If we really look at what a toddler experiences we surely realise they have such little control over their own lives, that it is no wonder that they get frustrated. Can you imagine how you would feel if you had such little control over your life? Is it really fair to call them 'manipulative' if they try to take control over just one tiny facet of their lives?

I believe that many rocky parent–toddler relationships can be traced back to the foundation of control, that of the parent having too much and the toddler too little. Of course I am not saying that you should give your toddler full control of their life: I fully appreciate it is not appropriate for them to walk around the supermarket naked or eat nothing but chocolate. Respectful parenting, however, is not about being permissive, it is about considering your toddler's needs and balancing them with your own, and it is about setting limits and boundaries and not being afraid to reinforce these in order to keep your toddler safe and healthy. You will find more about this in chapter 13.

Allowing your toddler some control over their life will not mean that they will 'always expect their own way' or 'find it difficult once they go to school and have to do what they are told', both being common concerns of parents, but I can promise you it will have a tremendously positive effect on their behaviour and in turn your relationship with them. It is ironic that in our fear of creating a demanding toddler we hold on so tightly to our control of them that we drive them to behave in ways that we do not like, all because of our well-meant misunderstanding.

Think back to the long-term goals you noted down in chapter 1; did you write that you hoped your toddler would grow into an adult who was confident, self-sufficient and capable of looking after themselves? Certainly once our children are at school we expect them to be able to do significantly more for themselves than we expected them to do as a toddler. By the time a child starts high school we certainly expect them to be able to remember their school bags, the right books and sports kit, we expect them to be in control of their homework, we expect them to get up and be dressed on time for school, we expect them to be able to prepare themselves simple food and drink and we certainly expect them to be able to tidy their rooms. This asynchrony of 'being in control' versus 'not being in control' is perplexing: when should a child be allowed control of their own life? When should we 'hand over the reins' to them? What is the best way to ensure that your toddler grows into a confident and self-reliant teen?

Setting the scene for tomorrow

If we allow our toddlers more control over their lives not only do we create a calmer, more harmonious relationship with them now, we are also setting the foundations for tomorrow. Giving your toddler some control shows them that you trust them; it shows that you respect them and the most sure-fire way of increasing their respect for you as their parent is first affording respect to them. The more we give toddlers appropriate ways of taking control, the less likely they are to try to take control in situations where we don't want them to.

How might this respect and allowance of control look in real life? It could be something as simple as allowing your toddler to choose their own clothes, within the boundaries you have set for them, and only you can decide if it is acceptable for them to wear a Spiderman costume five days per week. It could be allowing your toddler to eat instinctively and choose when they would prefer to eat their breakfast. It could be allowing your toddler to make the decision of where to go today. It could be allowing your toddler to decide when to wean from the breast or bottle or when to begin potty training. There are so many different ways to afford your toddler more control over their lives that it would look different for every family; there is no one 'right way' to help your toddler to have a little more control.

The importance of free play

Perhaps one of the most important areas of a toddler's life where you can let them have more control is through play. The term 'free play' is common now in the childcare industry, but what does it really mean? Think about how we might unintentionally control our child's play. As parents we totally dominate our toddler's play, for example by directing what they do by saying things like 'That piece of the jigsaw needs to go the other way up', steering the toys that they play with, 'You don't want to play with that old dolly, use the nice new one you got for your birthday' and choosing the time that they play, 'Let's get your building blocks out now'. How many times have you told your toddler things like, 'No, you need the green crayon, trees aren't blue', 'The square shape doesn't fit into the round hole, put it in the shape over there' or 'Dinosaurs don't live on a farm, put the dinosaur toy away and get the toy cows out'? I know I have. These comments are all well meaning; we are trying to help our children to learn and acquire knowledge about the world that they live in.

When we try to control our toddler's play, however, our words and actions can have the opposite effect to that desired, and we may accidentally inhibit our toddler's drive to explore the world as 'little scientists' and we may leave them feeling helpless to even play in the way they would like.

If your child is allowed to have full control over their play, and by this I mean they choose what they play with, when they play with it, how they play with it and who plays with them, if anyone, it can often have tremendously positive effects on their general behaviour. Play is the one part of their day when a toddler can truly be in control, in a world where they have no control over anything else. Allowing your child the freedom to enjoy free play also shows them that you respect them and if you engage in play with them, if they invite you to, you will be building their communication and cooperation skills in ways that you never could be when you are 'teaching' them.

The way toddlers play may seem strange and curious to us as adults, but play is the most important way that your toddler learns about the world or, as Albert Einstein famously said, 'play is the highest form of research'. Toddlers have wonderful imaginations and see the world in ways in which we have long forgotten; this is the beauty and marvel of allowing them to play in the way that they choose, in a world where dinosaurs can easily be cows, boxes can be castles, aluminium foil can be oceans and buttons can be stars.

Why toddlers love repetition

You may have noticed that your toddler likes to repeat the same play over and over. To us as adults this can be infuriating, particularly if your toddler has invited you to play the same imaginary game for the tenth day in a row, but this repetition provides him with a great source of comfort. This links to what we know about toddlers forming schemas, which we looked at in chapter 2. This constant repetition is how toddlers learn about the world and build confidence in themselves. Although we may be tempted to keep suggesting new things with the intention that our toddlers can learn more and have more enriched experiences it is important to follow your toddler's lead and need for repetition.

The ToddlerCalm™ daily playtime solution

In ToddlerCalm™ classes we suggest to parents that they try to enjoy five to ten minutes of uninterrupted free play with their toddlers daily. In reality this means telling your toddler that you can play with them if they would like you to, allowing them to choose the activity and involve you as they see fit. For younger toddlers this may look more like them playing and you playing alongside them, commenting on what they are doing, by using the descriptive praise we discussed in chapter 5. Let your toddler know when the playtime is coming to an end and ensure that they know playtime will happen again tomorrow if they get upset when it's over. Some families like to use egg timers so that their toddler can see how much time they have left; some set alarms on watches and the like. The aim of your playtime will be to give your toddler 100 per cent of your attention and let them take full control of the session. Enabling your toddler to feel more connected and in control in this way can work wonders for avoiding conflict at other times, as well as being a grounding experience for you as a parent. It may feel a little strange to play with your toddler in this way initially, but you will soon settle into a pattern and free playtime can quickly become as rewarding for parents as it is for toddlers.

When I run ToddlerCalm™ workshops with parents I'm always pleased to hear quite how many different suggestions they come up with themselves in order to allow their toddler a little more control; sometimes these suggestions are based upon ideas they plan to use in the future and sometimes they are based on things they already do with their toddlers. Sophie's story overleaf is a great example of somebody already allowing their toddler to have a little more control in order to enjoy a more peaceful relationship with them and an easier experience of toilet training.

Sophie's story

I had it in my mind that when my daughter was ready to stop having nappies she would herself initiate the transition, and so I hadn't made any plans to potty train as such. In order to be prepared I bought some knickers for her, and a potty and seat for the toilet, which she was aware of. She usually followed my husband and myself to the toilet when we went and I had talked to her about the idea that if she wanted to she could use the toilet and have knickers instead of nappies, but aside from that we hadn't emphasised any need for a change to happen.

One day, when she was about two and a half, she told me that she wanted to wear knickers. From that day on, through her choice, she didn't have a nappy any more except at night-time. At first I became quite tense and frustrated – I had assumed that waiting until she was ready would minimise accidents and she would somehow know what to do regarding needing the toilet. I soon realised that even though she felt ready, she still needed the time and space to understand her body and how to control her need to go to the toilet. I didn't change our days or activities, and we carried on as usual, but in the first few days I would frequently check with her if she needed the potty, and would start to feel a sense of despair when there were accidents – I felt as though I was constantly dealing with clothes and carpets soaked in wee! I realised though that this was something that she needed to feel in control of herself, and as soon as I adjusted my perception of my role in things to 'accident clean up lady' (I bought some Dettol spray, plenty of paper towels and always had lots of spare clothes handy) things were a lot better. I stepped back and said to her that I wouldn't ask any more, and that if she needed to go, just to let me know. After this the accidents massively decreased, and it only took a couple of weeks for her to be virtually accident free for both wees and poos. Giving her control and trusting her in the process, I realised that I didn't actually need to do anything myself, and that just by giving her the opportunity she was able figure it out for herself.

Eight weeks on, I usually invite her to go to the toilet with me when I go, usually first thing in the morning and before we go out somewhere, and sometimes she does, other times she doesn't, depending on if she needs to. We don't have any problems using public toilets or toilets at other people's houses, and we just did a transatlantic trip for ten days without any problems. She still has a nappy at night, although she is dry in the morning – when we tried without it made her worried in the night that she was going to need the toilet and it disrupted her sleep, and she wanted to have her nappy again. I am sure in time she will let us know when she no longer wants to have it.

Chapter 7

The RHYTHM of life

While we try to teach our children all about life,
our children teach us what life is all about.

Angela Schwindt, author

Most adults like to live in a predictable world, as being able to predict 'what comes next' gives us a sense of security. Our lives are governed by schedules and routines, from the rising and setting of the sun to the timings of our working day, the times we eat and the time that we go to bed to sleep. We have a 'working week', usually consisting of Monday to Friday, and a weekend that is a time for fun and relaxation. We use calendars and diaries to plan our social lives and appointments; we know that it is usually warm in the summer months and cold in the winter and we plan holidays around these months accordingly. We budget according to 'pay day', and we attend classes and clubs on the same day each week, just as we know that our favourite show is on television at the same day and time: all these regular occurrences help us to plan our lives and feel in control.

We live in a routine-based world and predictability helps us to feel secure; sometimes the routine may bore us and we yearn for a change, but without it we would feel confused and we almost certainly would miss the stability that it brings. Toddlers are no different; in fact they need this predictability even more than we do, and without it they too feel confused and insecure, and this confusion and insecurity can very quickly escalate into bigger feelings, culminating in tantrums and other behaviours that we, as adults, find inappropriate.

What might life be like with no predictability?

Imagine waking one day and having no idea what day it was; imagine also that there were no watches or clocks, and you had no way of telling what time it was as well as not knowing the day or date. Not only do you not know what day or time it is, imagine too that you have no way of knowing what is going to happen today until your partner pulls up outside your house and motions for you to get into the car. You are driven to a local meeting hall and told that there are lots of people for you to make friends with inside. You have no idea how long you are going to stay there for or when you are going to be picked up. You feel very nervous; being in a strange room with all of these new people is overpowering enough, but having no concept of how long you will be staying there or when your partner will be back to pick you up makes you more anxious. Finally your partner comes back and you are driven to the swimming pool and told 'It's time for your swimming lesson.' Again you have no idea how long the swimming will last for, when your partner is coming back or what you are doing afterwards. You feel very uncomfortable with the lack of predictability of your day, made even worse by the fact that you have no idea what day or time it is and how much of the day there is left or how much has passed.

I know that seems far-fetched, but this above scenario is precisely the sort of day our toddlers have, almost every day. They don't understand the concept of time, most don't understand days of the week or the seasons or months, or the fact that if they are at nursery on some days they get to stay at home, perhaps on public holidays, and some days they don't. Imagine how unsettling it must be for a toddler to be in a routine of daily nursery sessions but then suddenly to be at home for two weeks for Christmas or Easter holidays? Many parents struggle to understand why their toddler's behaviour deteriorates over holiday periods, but when you consider that they have lost all of the daily rhythm that helps them to feel secure, perhaps it isn't quite so surprising.

When routines can be good for toddlers

Many adults struggle with spontaneity. For example, I am a planner, I cannot bear people visiting me unannounced, I hate last minute arrangements and I'm very uncomfortable with unexpected changes to my daily routine. I like to live with the security of knowing what will happen today, tomorrow, next week and next month. I like to look at my diary on Sunday evening and know what is happening in the week ahead. This is what makes me secure. Why do we fail to understand that toddlers need this same stability to their lives? Given their lack of comprehension of calendars and clocks it would make sense that they need this predictability even more than adults. Very often, unsettled toddlers are those who have no rhythm or routine to their lives. I don't like to use the word 'routine' here actually as it brings to mind rigid instructions from experts who tell you when your child should sleep, how long they should sleep for and what you should be doing while they are sleeping. The 'routines' I am talking about, however, are different; they are natural routines that are unique to you and your child, routines that reassure you both, routines that help your toddler to feel confident and secure. Importantly, these routines are flexible, that is the timings and locations may change but the patterns and rhythms don't. These predictable routines and the knowledge of 'what comes next' helps your toddler to develop confidence and ensures that they feel secure enough in their day-to-day life to explore the wider world.

As adults, we tend to take the idea of having a rhythm to our day for granted and don't really question the concept of being able to predict our day in giving us a general sense of safety and security. But being able to predict our day does give us a much needed sense of comfort. Think how unsettling it is when you forget to put your watch on in the morning and have to spend the day not knowing what time it is to understand this idea. Having a predictable rhythm in their life gives a toddler a sense of being in control and as we saw in the previous chapter this sense of being in control will in turn reduce the need for less appropriate behaviours, which seek to take more control.

The other side of understanding the importance of rhythm in your toddler's life is realising that these rhythms need to be flexible, which is the key difference between natural, reassuring rhythms and rigid routines favoured by many experts. You need to be able to deviate slightly from the planned day ahead if your toddler is feeling under the weather or just simply in need of quiet one-to-one time with you. If your toddler wakes one morning and it is apparent that they are in need of a duvet day with you don't be afraid to cancel nursery or playgroup for that day. If your toddler seems tearful and you have a playdate arranged for that afternoon don't be embarrassed to put your toddler's needs first and reschedule the playdate for another day. The key to providing reassuring rhythms for your toddler is to be led by them and to be flexible.

Having a predictable rhythm is even more important to a toddler if the rest of their life is full of change. Perhaps you may have just moved house, perhaps you have been on holiday or perhaps a new baby may have arrived, but whatever the change one of the keys to keeping your toddler as secure as possible and helping them to navigate the change as easily as possible is to provide as much of a constant in their life as you can, and keeping their daily rhythm can reassure them that everything is OK, that they are safe and secure. The bigger the change in a toddler's life the more their need for control and predictability in their daily rhythms grows.

Why are toddlers better behaved for other people?

Many parents have commented to me that their toddlers are difficult for them but angels for nursery staff; they often take this to mean that their toddler prefers the nursery workers to their own mother or father. Parents then wonder what they have done wrong to damage the bond with their child and question whether their toddler really loves them. This can be a very destructive pattern of thought indeed that tends to reflect very negatively on almost every element of life with the child. In turn these feelings cause the parent to question other behaviour and perhaps the toddler picks up on these feelings and feels unease with them, causing their behaviour to deteriorate as a result.

In reality though, this scenario is almost always a good sign. Yes I did say it was good, you didn't read that incorrectly. How could this ever be good? What if I said that this behaviour is very often a sign that your toddler feels comfortable and safe in your presence? Very often the safety of your company and the rhythm of their predictable home life after a busy day at nursery may mean that toddlers feel safe to effectively offload. What do they offload? The stress of the day, anything that worried them, times when they felt overwhelmed, be that through something positive or negative, and the times when they missed you. Think back to the smoke in the bungalow example from chapter 2. That is what they need to unload and they need you, somebody they trust, to help them to do it. Now that they are safe with you in their predictable environment they feel secure enough to release these emotions in your presence. Their behaviour around you is far from indicating that they don't like you; it is the very opposite. Their behaviour shows you just how much they love you and just how safe you make them feel to be their authentic selves. What they need from you is your love and reassurance and you in turn need to realise just what a fantastic parent you are for allowing them to release any stress in your company and for building such a good relationship with them for them to trust you so implicitly.

How might providing more of a rhythm for your child's life look in practice? It could be doing the same things in the same order each day, for instance singing a song while tooth-brushing, then moving on to getting dressed with a special game, turn-taking or another song before going downstairs for breakfast. If your toddler goes to nursery or preschool you might get their bags and shoes out ready for nursery the day before, thus helping your toddler to understand that 'tomorrow is a nursery day'. If a new sibling has just been born, trying to fit your baby into your existing life, by carrying the newborn in a sling, will really help, while keeping your toddler's routines as normal as possible to help give them some security at a time that they often find very unsettling. Don't be tempted to stray too much from their usual day-to-day routine by sending them off to relatives, keeping them at home from nursery (unless they indicate that they want to stay with you) or relaxing bedtime hours.

It may be that having a regular bedtime routine with the same actions and ritual at a similar time each night is more important than the actual timing. Look again at the ToddlerCalm™ three step bedtime ritual in chapter 3. It seems that many parents struggling with their toddler's sleep have no rhythm to bedtime and the introduction of a simple routine can have amazing results.

Faye's story

We started Rosa's bedtime routine somewhere between her fourth and sixth month, when she was consistently in a rhythm of sleeping for a long period at night and just napping during the day. When we first started her bedtime routine she would have a bath, then we would put her nappy and pyjamas on and read one short book to her, after this she would have her milk, from either a bottle or breast depending on who was putting her to bed, lastly we would sing to her until she fell asleep and then put her into her cot where she would stay happily until after we went to bed. We would then bring her into bed with us at some point during the night.

Now that she is two and a half years old the routine has changed slightly over time. Now at about 6pm we try always to stop everything else and give her a bath with lavender in, or we might read books, do puzzles or something else quiet for a while. Then at about 6.30pm we brush her teeth and give her asthma inhaler. After this she chooses three books and we get her pyjamas and nappy on. She then gets into her bed and drinks her milk while I read her the stories she has chosen. If she isn't already asleep by the time the stories are finished I sing some songs to her. If, after this, she still isn't asleep I tell her, 'We've had our stories and songs and milk now, it's time for you to go to sleep or read your books if you're not tired yet.' She then will read in her bed for a while and go to sleep by herself, while I go and have dinner or whatever else I need to do. I always leave her door wide open so that there is light for her to read by and so that she knows if she needs to she can come to me or I can come to her. (I live in a flat so there is no danger of her falling downstairs.)

In Rosa's lifetime we have lived in five different places. Her routine has been all over the place other than at bedtime because my partner works shifts as a carer. I attend university full time, so sometimes I'm with her all day for a few days in a row while at other times I don't see her at all for a few days. She has also always spent a fair amount of time sleeping over at her grandparents and other family members' houses, but despite this bedtime normally goes pretty smoothly because she has the consistency of her bedtime routine. I think it is also important to point out that when there is some sort of occasion that means her bedtime routine completely goes out of the window for a day or so, having her bedtime routine afterwards helps her to get back into going to bed at her usual time very quickly.

Lastly, she has recently begun a phase of resisting anything I ask her to do and she does say 'No, I don't want to go to bed', when I say that it is bedtime, but once we've started the first step of her bedtime routine, which is brushing her teeth, she then does the rest of it without any trouble because she is so used to all of the things happening in that order.

Chapter 8

UNDERSTANDING the real problem

We spend the first 12 months of our children's lives teaching them to walk and talk and the next 12 months teaching them to sit down and shut up.

Phyllis Diller, comedienne

Most of the parenting books I read when my oldest child was a toddler gave me the impression that all toddlers were naughty, and that their tantrums were the result of them testing my boundaries and trying to manipulate me in some way. Night-time wakings were apparently indicative of them having formed bad habits, or again trying to make me do what they wanted, to let them sleep in my bed or stay up until midnight. I read that I needed to take a firm hand with their eating habits and that their reluctance to try new foods and eat their vegetables was again their way of trying to eat nothing but what they wanted all day. In order to fix these problems I was to ignore the bad behaviour and praise or reward the good; this then was supposed to 'fix' my toddler and we would live happily ever after.

We have already looked at the limitations of rewards and punishments when it comes to coping with toddler behaviour that we find challenging, and we have already gained a good understanding of a toddler's brain development and the biology of sleep and eating. What we need to do now is to apply this knowledge to our parenting skills and look deeper at our toddler's behaviour, to understand why they are behaving in the way that they are and to understand what the real problem or need is. For it is when we deal with the root cause that we have a real chance of making a difference.

The problem with labelling toddlers

In ToddlerCalm™ classes we always highlight to parents that no toddlers are inherently naughty, and no toddler is born manipulative or destructive, and we then help them to understand that what they are really unhappy with is their toddler's behaviour, not the toddler him or herself. This is something I will discuss in a later chapter, but for now though I would like to focus on the idea of trying to understand our toddlers, to understand what is driving them to act in the way that we find unacceptable. When we consider that a toddler is tantruming for a reason that is possibly very upsetting to them, our responses to our toddler become very different, as I've mentioned before. So, rather than viewing your toddler as 'giving' you a hard time, consider that they are 'having' a hard time instead.

I was shopping recently and I noticed, as I was browsing the rails in a local clothing store, a stressed mother and her young daughter, aged about three, standing next to me. The toddler was clearly very bored and was complaining of being tired too. She asked her mother, politely, if they could go home, but the mother ignored her. The girl asked again. Remember how we saw what an important skill persistence is for toddlers right at the start of this book? This little girl was a great example of this and she asked for a third time, though by now it was very apparent that she was fed up with being ignored, indeed who wouldn't be? Her polite tone had now changed to whining. Her mother responded flippantly by telling her to 'Wait, just be quiet, we won't be long.' The girl looked so sad at this point; her needs were being totally ignored and she was clearly shattered. A full-scale tantrum ensued, big fat tears rolling down the little girl's face, and now she had her mother's attention, but not in the way that she wanted.

Now she was being shouted at and her already fragile state deteriorated even more as her mother told her to 'stop being so selfish' and to 'stop acting up'. At this point both mother and daughter were full of anger, stress, anxiety and sadness; they were almost feeding off each other's negative emotions. Sadly, on this particular occasion the toddler was dragged out of the shop and told that they were 'going home now, you always get your own way, I'm sick of it'. This scenario is so common. I know that I have ignored my own children's needs on many an occasion and then I blamed them for being spoilt, selfish or manipulative, when in reality they were none of these things, they just needed something I couldn't or wasn't prepared to give them.

Parenting is hard; certainly it is the hardest thing I have ever done. It really is hard to pause before you act and to try to think rationally and with empathy when your first instinct may be to snap, but if you can take just a moment to try to understand your toddler's behaviour things ultimately will be easier for both of you. This may mean that you need to postpone your shopping trip or cope with some other such inconvenience, but it also means you won't have to deal with the trauma of an out of control toddler, with your own feelings spiralling rapidly out of control too. When we label toddlers as 'naughty', 'troublesome' or 'manipulative' we don't see the real issue, we miss the most important thing of all, our toddler's individuality and our toddler's feelings. No toddler is really any of these things and by labelling them as such at best we become blind to the real reasons for their behaviour and at worst we set them up for years of issues with self-confidence and belief.

What is your toddler feeling?

A couple of years ago I was exhibiting at a large baby and toddler show. The exhibition centre was packed with thousands of parents and stall-holders alike, loud music was booming from the stage, buggies were everywhere, the room was stiflingly hot and bright spotlights were glaring down from the ceiling and stalls. It was an environment I hated; each day I went home feeling exhausted, my head throbbing, my feet aching, my ears ringing. I am an adult though, so if it was that unpleasant for me, imagine how it must have been for a two-year-old, being dragged around seeing nothing but a sea of legs and buggy wheels or sitting in buggies looking up at the bright spotlights, hearing the thumping music with their delicate young ears. Many parents who stopped at our stall commented to me that their baby or toddler was very unsettled and they didn't know why. To me it was obvious, but I suppose it is only really so if you know what you are looking for. It was no surprise then that several of the parents commented that their babies were 'being difficult, trying to spoil my fun' or that their toddlers were 'being really naughty today'. Indeed, I have felt like that myself many times before I really tried to understand what it must be like to be a toddler.

With this in mind, the next time your toddler tantrums because you won't let them have an ice cream, try to think about how disappointed they might feel. Consider how you might feel if you were hungry and saw your favourite food but were told you couldn't have it. I am not saying that you should always 'give in' to your toddler and buy them the ice cream, far from it; boundaries are important and being permissive will not help anybody. There will be more on this in chapter 13 but for now understand that it's OK to say 'no', just accompany that 'no' with some compassion for how sad your toddler might be feeling and instead of chastising them for being 'naughty' when the obvious tantrum ensues, consider hugging them and empathising instead, perhaps saying something like 'Darling, you really wanted that ice cream didn't you? You must be so sad that Mummy said no, I'm so sorry.'

The next time that your toddler wakes in the night and cries for you, in your sleep-deprived haze, try to think about how it feels when you have a nightmare or go to bed after a particularly scary movie, how you like reassurance then too, whether it be a hug from your partner or sleeping with the lamp on. The next time your toddler whines for a new toy, think about how it feels to be shopping and see a handbag that you fall in love with but know that you can't have, imagine the disappointment you feel and know that your toddler feels disappointed too. Recognising these feelings can help you to stay calm and your reaction will help your toddler to feel that their emotions are being validated.

Understand your toddler's biological limitations

Toddlers are not the same as adults; they think differently, feel differently, eat differently and sleep differently, so with this in mind why do we expect them to behave in adult ways? Why do we expect them to sleep through the night, clear their plates, share their toys and understand lengthy, rational explanations of why they must 'be good'? I think society overestimates toddlers, but not in a good way. We overestimate their social skills, we overestimate their use of complicated mental skills such as logical reasoning and empathy, and we overestimate their ability to soothe themselves. If we adjust our expectations of toddlers, based on an accurate understanding of their neuropsychology, then we can avoid many of the struggles parents of toddlers face on a daily basis. Science tells us that it is entirely normal for toddlers to act impulsively without really thinking their actions through, because of their immature brain development. When your toddler grabs a toy off another at playgroup, and perhaps shoves the other toddler in the process, he is not being 'naughty'; he is behaving in a perfectly normal and indeed expected way for his age.

Societal rules and toddler behaviour

Unfortunately, society's incorrect expectations of a toddler's physical and mental skills lead parents to feel embarrassed about their toddler's normal behaviour. They feel it is something they should apologise for and be seen to act on and discipline in public, for fear of being perceived a 'bad' or permissive parent, even if the discipline is performed in such a way that is completely at odds with their toddler's brain development, such as making the toddler apologise for snatching a toy, for example. We know that toddlers do not have a fully formed sense of empathy, therefore making them apologise to another toddler is meaningless, as the toddler does not understand what is happening and will certainly not learn from the event, yet it is something as parents we feel we must do for fear that our toddler's behaviour will reflect negatively on us and through concern that our toddler must learn to be nice. We need to realise that these expectations and needs are all our own, as adults.

Quite often our feelings and behaviours are completely at odds with what a toddler feels and really needs, yet our society has become so warped in our expectations of toddlers that in our quest to raise more sociable children we actually behave in a way that is likely to make them less so. The following quote from psychologist C. G. Jung sums this idea up very well, 'If there is anything we wish to change in the child, we should first examine it and see whether it is not something that could be better changed in ourselves.'

When I refer to 'understanding the real problem' in the title of this chapter this applies to understanding ourselves as well as our toddlers. Sometimes as parents we need to realise when we are acting on a need of our own, rather than one of our toddler's, and if this is the case our best response would be to try to control our own behaviour and response to our toddler rather than punishing our toddler. In chapter 12 we will look at this in much more detail when we look at the concept of unconditional love, but I would like to sow a small seed of thought now. Does the key to a calmer toddlerhood lie in controlling our own behaviour, as parents, rather than trying to control our toddler's behaviour?

I think it is always helpful to gain a good understanding of the reasons and causes behind your own child's behaviour, but for some parents this understanding is even more important.

Jane's story

Our youngest daughter Jessica was ten months old when her sister Ruby took a toy from her while I was preparing dinner. I heard the upset cry, followed by a thud. I dashed into the living room to find Jessica seemingly lifeless and blue on the living room floor.

I shook her and frantically shouted for her to wake up, and Ruby, then two years old, was also asking her to wake up, but with no response. With my mobile phone lost and the house phone lacking enough charge to make a call I grabbed Jessica and ran outside shouting in the street in the hope that a neighbour would hear my calls for help. Nothing, as everybody was at work. We returned inside again and after around one minute Jessica began to breathe once again. It felt like a lifetime.

We visited the doctors the following day and received a diagnosis of 'possible breath holding syndrome'. I was also told that breath holding was not uncommon and that Jessica would eventually grow out of it.

A fortnight later it happened again, at the same sort of time of day, which was just before bath-time, and with the same trigger, which was Jessica getting upset over something. This time though I was with her when it happened and saw that she cried, then almost gasped for breath, resulting in her turning blue very quickly, before finally falling to the floor. She was unconscious for the same sort of time as the first occurrence and again I was on my own with the children when it happened.

The breath holding incidents then began to occur two or three times a week and my husband, who works shifts and had missed the first two occasions, was finally able to observe what was happening.

We quickly learnt that we needed to try to stop the trigger, which was Jessica getting upset in the late afternoon. This meant we needed to pay particular attention to her, especially at her trigger time, try to keep her happy and not to leave our two girls alone together for too long, to prevent any squabbles that would set off Jessica's condition.

The breath holding incidences terrified me and, aware of a previous diagnosis she had received of a heart murmur, I did some research and came across something known as RAS (reflex anoxic seizures). I found a little girl's story, which was very similar to Jessica's, but after another doctor's visit this idea was dismissed after a listen to Jessica's heart.

Then, one day in December, when Jessica was eighteen months old, she had another incident, but this time she stopped breathing for approximately three minutes. My husband called for an ambulance while I performed CPR on her to keep the oxygen pumping around her body. I wasn't sure whether her heart had stopped or not, but I was thankful for the first aid training I'd done just a fortnight before. When the paramedics arrived, Jessica was unconscious, but her physical observations, such as pulse, oxygen saturation and temperature, were all normal. We stayed in hospital overnight that evening as a precaution.

I still felt we needed more answers. We returned to the doctor for the third time and finally, at nineteen months old, Jessica was referred to see a consultant paediatric cardiologist. She had an echocardiogram (an ultrasound of the heart) and after a quick review, the cardiologist ruled out my earlier suspicions of RAS and explained that her symptoms were indeed classic signs of 'baby holding breath syndrome', which we are told she will grow out of by the time she is around four years old.

Jess has had many incidents since, and to add to the breath holding resulting in unconsciousness, now she is toilet trained we have also learnt that when she has an attack she loses all control of her bladder, so we have to be prepared there too.

Jessica is now two-and-a-half years old and we've noticed that the breath holding incidences are becoming less frequent, and she now has one every couple of months or so. As soon as we hear of any upset late in the day, wherever we are, we pay attention to her very quickly and try to respond to her needs. It is getting easier though, especially now that we can see the light at the end of the tunnel.

Chapter 9

COMMUNICATION – toddler style

Don't worry that children never listen to you.
Worry that they are always watching you.

Robert Fulghum, author

How do our toddlers communicate with us and how do we communicate with our toddlers? Those are pretty big questions, but I don't think we give enough thought to them. First we will look at how toddlers communicate with us.

How do toddlers communicate with us?

When we think about communication we often think of it as verbal only, i.e. the words we speak. This is only the beginning though. Communication encompasses the way we say things, the tone and volume of our voice, and other non-language based noises we make such as laughter, crying and sighing. Naturally body language is a huge communication tool too with gestures such as smiling, frowning, eye widening, grimacing, head turning and eye contact, or removal of eye contact, all being forms of communication. A dictionary definition of communication is 'the activity of conveying information through the exchange of thoughts, messages, or information, as by speech, visuals, signals, writing, or behaviour'. When we think of communication in the true sense of the word, then we understand that it goes way beyond speech.

Many people believe toddlers have difficulty communicating, based largely on their immature speech development, and certainly we know that the first three years of life are an incredibly busy period with respect to language acquisition. Around a child's first birthday they are expected to be using one or more words with meaning; by eighteen months this expectation rises to somewhere between five and twenty words; by the child's second birthday we expect anywhere in the region of a hundred and fifty to three hundred words; and by the time a child turns three we expect in the region of a staggering one thousand words. Many of these words, somewhere around ten to thirty per cent, however, will still be unintelligible, with adults not able to understand what the toddler is saying. Along with the acquisition of words for themselves, toddlers are also learning to understand words spoken by others, they are learning the principles of grammar and turn taking in communication, as well as learning how to describe, compare and contrast and verbalise their internal feelings. If we consider what a toddler is learning it is absolutely mind blowing. In comparison to an adult, however, a toddler's verbal communication skills are clearly under-developed.

Does this immature verbal ability render toddlers unable to communicate with us though? The answer of course is absolutely not. Have you ever wondered how animals communicate with each other without speech? If the problems we have with our toddlers were due to their immature communication skills surely every other species on the planet would struggle as much with their young as we do with ours, perhaps even more so. Perhaps then a toddler's lack of speech is not really the problem we make it out to be. What if the real problem was that our toddlers were communicating clearly to us, but we were blind to their communication?

Tantrums as a communication tool

Many toddlers frequently tantrum, yet this is absolutely not acceptable to society, which views it as a behaviour that should be stopped as soon as possible. Toddlers tantruming, especially in public, are seen as ill behaved, poorly disciplined, manipulative and destructive, and indeed many parenting experts believe that tantrums are something to be nipped in the bud as quickly as possible. What if I said though that tantrums are a valid form of communication for toddlers and that silencing them is as disrespectful as telling a child to 'be quiet' in mid-flow of conversation? We may not like toddler tantrums, we may feel embarrassed by them, we may feel the need to act appropriately for fear of society's expectations and reactions, they may make us uncomfortable, they may make us angry, but nevertheless they are a perfectly valid form of communication for toddlers.

When a toddler tantrums it is a culmination of their big feelings, whether they may be fear, sadness, anger or something else, combined with their under-formed brain's inability to control their impulses to react. A tantruming toddler is one communicating to us in a big way; they are telling us that they need our help, and that they are feeling overwhelming emotions they cannot handle on their own. With this in mind why would we sit them on a naughty step or put them in 'time out' to 'calm down'? It just doesn't make sense, does it, outside of the fact that we don't really understand how our toddlers are feeling, that we are too wrapped up in societal expectations and the warnings of the experts who tell us this behaviour must stop. Tantrums are communication and isn't all communication from our toddlers worth listening to?

How about other forms of communication your toddler may use? Examples might be grimacing and turning their head away from a spoonful of food, clinging to your leg and crying at nursery drop-off, frowning and hitting out when another child takes the toy they wanted at playgroup, grabbing items off the shelves in shops, biting another child on a playdate, averting their gaze from yours when you are telling them off and banging their head on the floor when they are told not to jump on the sofa. Every single one of these instances is a toddler communicating to us. I appreciate that many of these are undesirable forms of communication that we need to steer toddlers away from, but they are communicating nevertheless.

In the case of the toddler grimacing and turning away from food they may be saying, 'I really don't like this, Mum, it tastes horribly bitter; please don't make me eat it.' In the case of the toddler clinging to your leg and crying at nursery drop-off they might be saying, 'Please don't make me go to nursery, I really need to be with you today, I really don't feel confident on my own.' When a toddler hits another child at playgroup they may want to say, 'That toy is mine, I don't want anyone else to play with it, I love it so much and I'm so mad at that little boy, he took the one thing I want most in the world.' In the case of grabbing items off shop shelves consider that the toddler might be thinking, 'Yum, that looks really good, I'm really hungry right now and I think that would really fill me up as well as looking really tasty.' When a toddler bites another child on a playdate they might want to say, 'I don't like sharing my space with this other child, or my toys; they are making me feel angry and overwhelmed, please can they go home.' When a toddler averts their gaze from you when you tell them off perhaps they are telling you, 'It makes me scared when you shout at me, I love you, please love me back' and when they bang their head on the floor after being told to not jump on the sofa they might be wanting to tell you, 'I loved doing that so much, it felt so fun to bounce up and down, I am so sad and so mad that you stopped my fun, I can't cope with how strong my feelings are.'

Of course I don't really know what toddlers think and their reasons for acting in the way they do are different in every single scenario for every single toddler, but what I do know is that in the vast majority of cases their actions are not meant to be 'naughty' or 'manipulative', instead they are most likely an indication of an unmet need or misunderstood feelings. Their actions are communication and commonly they are communicating a cry for our help in order to regulate their emotions and big feelings. Why, then, don't we just give them this help? Why do we view most common toddler behaviours as 'naughty'; why do we chastise them for their feelings? If we did view their actions as valid communication and responded appropriately I can almost guarantee that we would find parenting toddlers a lot easier. If toddlers feel respected and listened to, so in turn their need for our attention will lessen, their ability to regulate their emotions will grow as a response to our compassion and nurturing and, soon enough, when their verbal development catches up, these behaviours will dramatically reduce. As a parent of a toddler one of our key roles is to understand that all behaviour is communication; our task is to try to understand what the communication is.

How do we communicate with toddlers?

Understanding our toddlers' communication and responding appropriately can have a huge positive impact on day-to-day life, but how we communicate with our toddlers can have a huge impact too, both positively and negatively.

As parents one difficulty we experience in communicating with toddlers is that we both view and experience the world in a very different way, so it is important that we adapt our communication, particularly verbal, when we speak to toddlers in order to maximise the toddler's chances of being able to both understand and listen. Very often communication problems between parents and toddlers can be due to the adult not understanding the need for them to adapt their communication appropriately.

It is important here to think back to what we know about the toddler brain, specifically their relatively immature neocortex. In chapter 2 we saw how the neocortex, the last part of the human brain to develop, is very under-developed in toddlers. When we consider that the neocortex is responsible for logical reasoning and rational thought it becomes obvious that reasoning with our toddlers, or giving them lengthy rational explanations for our requests, is almost entirely pointless, because they just won't understand us. Similarly, if we remember that our toddlers do not fully understand the concept of empathy we begin to understand how pointless it is to get them to apologise for any 'wrongdoing'.

Toddlers respond best to simple, clear, positive language that is aimed at their level. Think too about your non-verbal communication: toddlers will respond better to a calm voice and an adult who speaks to them at their eye level. Imagine how threatening it feels when someone with authority over you is towering above you and raising their voice, would this make you more or less inclined to listen to them? The same is true for your toddler, so bending down to his level, maintaining eye contact and speaking in a soft voice is far more likely to have a positive effect than shouting.

Parents as role models

We have already looked at the work of Albert Bandura and his 'social learning theory' (remember the Bobo dolls) in chapter 2, and what Bandura clearly showed us was that toddlers are great mimics; they learn from our behaviour and they copy us. Our toddlers are our greatest mirrors, so if you see behaviour you do not like in your toddler it is always worth considering where the behaviour came from, and sadly it is often from us, the toddler's parents. I certainly shout too much at my children; in fact I always know if I have had a particularly shouty spell as that is exactly what my children mirror back at me. Perhaps one of the easiest ways to reduce unwanted behaviour in our children is to consider how we behave ourselves.

Toddler communication tips

The following is a list of suggestions that could help both you and your toddler to communicate with each other a little more effectively. Of course, this list is just the start, as I'm sure you will find you do some of these things already, and perhaps you may do some effective things that are not on here.

• Limit the number of commands you give at the same time, as too many will confuse your toddler: 'Get your socks from your bedroom, put your shoes on and then come to the kitchen for breakfast' is just too much at once. One command at a time is usually enough.

- Allow your toddler time to process what they have just heard; it might take them a good few moments to comprehend what you've said and then filter through to new behaviour.

- Say what you do want rather than what you don't want. For instance, 'walking feet please' is much more effective than 'stop running'; very often toddlers only focus on one command, and in the case of 'stop running' it is almost always the 'running' part they will listen to!

- Speak in a calm voice, remembering that as parents we need to model the behaviour we want to see in our child.

- Toddlers use visual communication clues much more than adults who rely predominantly on verbal communication. For instance getting a towel and some bubble bath out could be used as a signal to your toddler that bath-time is coming up soon.

- Help toddlers to identify their feelings. For instance, 'It really made you sad when we had to leave the park didn't it?' shows the child that you have recognised their feelings and helps them to feel validated, while also helping them to name their big feelings so that when they have the verbal capacity to do so they can talk about their feelings with you.

- Say what you see. If you see your child fighting with another child over a toy you might say, 'I see that you both want to play with the ball.' This helps your toddler to know that you understand his feelings.

- Say what you saw. After the struggle with another child you might say, 'You really wanted the ball didn't you, but the little boy took it away from you.' This helps the child to understand what has happened and process the event in their own minds, as well as validating their feelings once more.

- Question your toddler. If you see your toddler struggling with something, asking them questions is far more useful than instructing them or giving them the answer. For instance, if they are struggling with a jigsaw puzzle you might say, 'What sort of shape needs to go there?', rather than 'Use the square piece.' This shows your toddler you understand their frustration but that you believe in their abilities to problem solve. In short it empowers them, rather than solving the problem yourself, which disempowers them.

- Talk to yourself out loud. Yes, you might feel a bit crazy, but this really is just a form of modelling; if your toddler is struggling with a puzzle you might say to yourself (but out loud), 'I'm sure Johnny will find the right puzzle piece.'

- Be respectful as much as possible. If your toddler doesn't want to share a toy with another child and answers with 'No', whenever you ask him to share, ask him if he can think of another solution. Perhaps you might suggest one through a question yourself, such as, 'What about if we use this egg timer to help? When the sand runs out you'll know when to swap toys.'

- Understand that toddler communication stretches well beyond verbal communication, so think what their behaviour is possibly indicating. Does your toddler have little gestures that indicate he might be tired? Hungry? If you can learn what these gestures mean you can often stop unwanted behaviour from happening.

- Never teach your child it is unacceptable to cry. Crying is important to us all; it is how we release hurtful emotions, and too many toddlers are told to 'be a big boy' or 'big girls don't cry'. If your toddler is encouraged to release his emotions through crying this is far less likely to manifest in unwanted behaviour because the hurtful feelings are retained inside.

- Never tell your child how they feel: 'Ssshhh it's all better, it doesn't hurt any more.' Far better to say, 'It seems like that really hurt you and you need to cry to calm down; it's OK I'm here while you do.'

Shelley's story

I first came across the concept of 'baby signing' around eight years ago. Baby signing is the concept of using sign language, with speech, to communicate with hearing babies and toddlers. Newly pregnant with my first baby, I was fascinated with the promise that my hearing baby would be calmer, with fewer tears and tantrums, if I learnt to use sign with her. Being of a rather sceptical nature, and having only come across sign language being used by people who were deaf, I embarked on my own fact-finding mission and, quite honestly, was astounded at what I discovered about the use of signing with hearing children. I was convinced enough to give it a try and started signing with my little girl a few weeks after she was born.

Several babies later, and I firmly believe in 'baby signing'. Signing with my children did mean that they were calmer. Not only that, they were more confident and more content. And I could meet their needs, quickly and without tantrums or tears because I knew straight away that they needed a nappy change, or something to eat, or that they were scared and wanted a cuddle. Or they just wanted to know 'Why?' They could also tell me what they wanted (which didn't necessarily translate to them having it, but at least I knew what was on their mind). Also, because we spent much less time having to 'manage' unwanted behaviour, we could spend more time having fun; getting to know each other and finding out about the joys that only toddlers can show you, such as jumping in puddles and spotting slugs.

One of my favourite memories of signing includes a time when my eldest daughter was seventeen months old and she brought over a picture of me at about fifteen years old to show me. She pointed to it and sort of said 'girl' by which I understood she was trying to say 'girl'. I explained it was a picture of me when I was little. I really didn't expect her to get the concept, but then she reached up her little hand, tapped my head twice to sign 'mummy' (which she had not done before) and pointed to the picture. Wow! If it wasn't for signing I would have never have known that she understood me or that she completely 'got' what I was trying to tell her.

Signing with toddlers is, in my opinion, imperative. When my middle daughter was nearly three, at the drop of a hat and for no seeming reason, she started resorting to tantrums. Her vocabulary was excellent; her use of language, for her age, astounding. She was a confident and articulate child most of the time, a common outcome with most signing babies. So, why the tantrums? Life was simply overwhelming for her. She couldn't cope with everything that assailed her senses on a daily basis and when she was tired, she lost the ability to communicate clearly what she wanted or what had upset her with speech. So, instead, I talked to her and asked her to show me, with her signs, how I could help her. It benefited us both: firstly, she had my absolute and undivided attention as I was completely focused on her to see her signs and, secondly, she could tell me that she needed a cuddle, that she was tired and wanted her bear. The storm passed, and calm was restored quickly and easily.

Of course you can tell whether a small child is hungry, tired or cold without the need for signing. But how else would I have known that my girls, aged between eighteen months and two and a half, would prefer a yoghurt to some grapes, that they needed the toilet (signing was the single most effective tool when we were toilet training), or that they were sad because they missed their daddy, who had gone away with work? All of this was conveyed without resorting to tantrums or getting to meltdown point. My eldest daughter was frequently upset in new environments or if we stayed somewhere too long and she could tell me that the reason she was upset wasn't just boredom or tiredness, but specifically that she wanted to go home as she had had enough. Sensory overload is a big trigger point for lots of small children but it was my ability to communicate with my children using sign language that highlighted this for me and enabled me to cope so much better during the toddler years. Quite simply, the guesswork disappeared and, as an added benefit, everyone in our family was able to join in with the 'conversation'.

A toddler wouldn't be speaking more extensively if they couldn't sign. They'd not only be not speaking but also be unable to communicate in any other way. Signing allows small children the ability to get their point across, to be understood and to have their needs met. I'm not the only parent in the world to experience these incredible interactions. Many parents have these dialogues with signing babies and toddlers; their internal life is far richer than their physical ability to speak allows them to share. For children with additional needs, signing allows them to connect and bond much sooner than they could without it.

I am an absolute convert to the benefits of using sign language, in conjunction with speech, with babies and young children. While I wouldn't go as far as to say that signing is a magic cure-all, it is an incredible preventive when done correctly, putting a stop to toddler frustration and upset very effectively. Best of all, signing can be put into place easily, quickly and at very little cost.

Chapter 10

Treating your toddler as an INDIVIDUAL

*Accept the children the way we accept trees –
with gratitude, because they are a blessing – but do
not have expectations or desires. You don't expect
trees to change; you love them as they are.*

Isabel Allende, author

Are you exactly the same as your siblings? Do you have the same likes and dislikes as your friends? It is universally acknowledged that all adults are different in their preferences and personalities; wouldn't it be a strange world if we all liked the same things? Imagine a restaurant with no menu, just set food that everybody ate, imagine if we all went on holiday to the same place, if we all liked the same music and read the same books. Imagine what the world would be like if we all went to bed at 10pm and rose at 7am. The world would be a very funny place indeed wouldn't it?

While we appreciate that all adults are unique, we often

expect our toddlers to all be the same, for instance, we expect them to all sleep for the average amount of time for their age and eat the average amount of food for their age and enjoy the same food as us. If our friend raves about a new playgroup and the fun that her toddler has there, of course we expect our toddler will like it too, and if we choose new clothing that we adore for our toddler we are perplexed when they refuse to wear it. Every toddler, however, is wonderfully, and often frustratingly, unique. Trying to fit our toddler into the mould of 'the toddler norm' is a potentially damaging act, damaging for them and for us. If our toddlers don't 'fit in' we often wonder what we have done wrong, and what could we have done differently in our parenting to make them more outgoing, confident, happy or adventurous.

I often meet parents who are very different to their toddlers and many times they view these differences as problems. I think this is most heightened among extrovert, confident parents who are quick to show their happiness, life's optimists, those who are the life and soul of the party and probably always have been. When these parents find that their toddlers do not take after them in this personality trait they can really be thrown, and they sometimes have trouble understanding why their toddler is so shy and so introverted and shows such little positive emotion in comparison to themselves. I often find these extrovert parents struggle to relate to their introvert children, wondering what they have done wrong to create such a quiet and seemingly unhappy child and trying all they can to make their toddler 'come out of their shell', which almost always never works.

In reality these parents have of course done nothing wrong; their toddler is probably perfectly happy, they just show it in a different way and react to situations differently to their parents. The real key for these parents is to understand that their toddler's emotions are still perfectly valid. If the toddler is shy in new situations and prefers the company of his mother to a room full of children the easiest thing to do as a parent is to accept that your child is an individual, that he feels and experiences the world in a different way to you and in turn he needs you to parent him differently from the way you were yourself parented. This quietness is not a flaw that needs to be changed, it is just the way your toddler is.

Once we accept our toddlers as unique individuals we can reset our expectations of them, which in turn will help to reset our relationships. Just because your friend's little girl was potty trained before her second birthday it doesn't mean that there is anything wrong with your little boy still being in nappies by his third birthday. Just because your sister's son sleeps for twelve hours straight per night it doesn't mean that there is anything wrong with your daughter waking every three hours. Just because the book you read told you that all children are ready for pre-school at two and a half it doesn't mean that your toddler will be; some toddlers benefit from staying at home with their parents until the age of four or five and beyond, while some thrive in the company of others shortly after their second birthday. One lesson I learnt very early on in my parenting journey was that comparing my children to others, including other children of my own, would generally only end in tears, and similarly comparing myself to other mothers was damaging too. The sooner I accepted myself and my children as individuals the happier we all became.

The problem with 'one size fits all' parenting

As well as your toddler possessing an entirely unique personality, it is also important to remember that their life experience and situation is completely unique too. With this in mind it makes it almost impossible to give standard 'toddler behaviour' advice. I am often asked questions such as 'What do you suggest for a toddler who bites?', 'How can I make my toddler sleep more?' or 'How can I stop my toddler being jealous of the new baby?' In all honesty I can't answer these questions; there are just too many variables to consider. I firmly believe that giving a 'one size fits all' answer for toddlers is naïve; no two toddlers are the same and therefore no two situations are the same either, which means it is impossible to give standard parenting advice. Each toddler and each parent needs to consider the best way forward for them and their way may be very different from that of a friend or relative, even if the situations superficially look the same.

I am saddened that this is a point that many toddler experts don't recognise. The 'one size fits all' answers often don't work or leave the toddler or parent (and frequently both) stressed and disempowered. For this reason I decided very early on in the development of ToddlerCalm™ that there was to be no 'ToddlerCalm™ way'. I vowed that all parents attending our courses would be treated as individuals and their toddlers and situations too; it is only when we truly understand this that we can begin to empower parents and help toddlers. Some toddlers need their parents more than others; some are ready to explore the world alone from a very early age. Some toddlers are happy to sleep alone every night; some need the close proximity of parents for several years. Some are ready to give up bottles or breastfeeding while still babies; some need the comfort and milk for many years. All toddlers are individuals. I cannot stress this highly enough. Remember that developmental guidelines are really only that, just guidelines, and there really is no 'normal' when it comes to toddlers (or humans of any age). Just because your friend's toddler is doing something it doesn't mean that there is a problem that your toddler isn't and vice versa.

Mind-mindedness parenting

Parents who treat their toddlers as individuals with minds of their own, and empathise with, value and validate their feelings and behaviour are almost always the most relaxed and happy, as are their toddlers. Psychologists give this concept a name: 'mind-mindedness'. In a sense mind-mindedness refers to a parent's ability to 'mind read' their child, not in a spiritual sense, but the idea that a parent recognises that their child is an individual who thinks and feels and tries to interpret what they may be thinking.

There has been much interest lately in what makes some parents more adept at mind-mindedness than others, and recent research[28] has focused on recording infant–parent interactions to try to answer this question. The results of this research rather surprisingly showed that mind-mindedness is seemingly unrelated to the socio-economic background and mental health of parents and also to the temperament of the child, but does appear to be related to the pregnancy and birth of the child. Those who had a planned and positive pregnancy and a positive recollection of the first moments with their child appeared more mind-minded than those who found the early experience more traumatic. As someone who has been heavily involved in the birth industry for many years this does not surprise me, particularly with the recent research into oxytocin (the hormone of love), which we will look at further in chapter 12. As a society our disinterest in the psychological effects of birth, viewing it as 'just one day in your life', is far-reaching and something that needs to change, quickly.

Further research[29] also indicates a link between mind-mindedness and the development of toddlers' abilities, particularly in relation to play and language development. The scientists also found that a big indicator of mind-mindedness in the toddler years is what happens in babyhood. Lead researcher, Dr Elizabeth Meins, comments, 'What we found is that if you try and see if there's a reason why your baby might be crying, rather than it simply being a random event, it might help you cope.' To me this just highlights again how important it is to view your toddler as an individual, to understand that they all have their own thoughts and feelings. If you understand this and can begin to imagine what your toddler may be feeling it can certainly help both of you to cope during periods of tricky behaviour. The real scientific understanding that is most needed is how to help parents to become more mind-minded, but sadly, to my knowledge, this research does not yet exist. I do think that a combination of education, changes in birth practices and baby raising practices (focusing on the release of oxytocin – see chapter 12) may hold the key.

If parents genuinely treated their children as individuals with minds of their own, preferably from babyhood, and stopped worrying about what they should be doing, life would be so much simpler. Afforded this respect, respect that they think and feel in their own unique ways, toddlers would have less need to fight for control or to tantrum to try to get themselves heard. As parents we would have different, more realistic, expectations of our toddlers. We wouldn't expect them to like something just because we do and we wouldn't expect them to be like us. We would view them as the fascinating, unique individual that they are and rejoice in some of the behaviour that drives us to tears at the moment.

I would like to sum up this chapter with a beautiful quote from psychotherapist Virginia Satir, as I feel that this is one of the key needs of toddlers and one of the most important, and sometimes hardest, points for parents to understand: 'Feelings of worth can flourish only in an atmosphere where individual differences are appreciated, mistakes are tolerated, communication is open, and rules are flexible – the kind of atmosphere that is found in a nurturing family.'

In my journey of working with parents I have met many whom I have deeply respected for the choices they have made.

I particularly respect those who are willing to buck the trend in modern day, Western society and bear the brunt of ridicule, judgement and criticism in order to treat their toddler as an individual and to do what they feel is best for their toddler's own unique needs. Lynsey is one of these parents. The irony is if Lynsey lived in another country, Mongolia for instance, her story would be the norm, but in the UK it is very far from it.

Lynsey's story

I don't remember having a 'plan' on how long I would breastfeed when I had my first baby over six years ago. My mum breastfed my sister and I can remember watching my mum feed her so it seemed totally normal to me. I didn't really consider much beyond the first six months when my milk was the only food my baby would need.

I recall a conversation with my husband during the early months of breastfeeding our son. I discovered the World Health Organisation recommends continuing to breastfeed up to or beyond two years and shared this with him. My husband said he felt a bit uncomfortable with the idea of a child older than one year being breastfed. I felt sad and a bit worried that he might not support me but looking at my little baby still being exclusively breastfed, it felt like it was a long way off and I would cross that bridge if and when we came to it.

As my baby's half-birthday approached he began sitting up and was able to pick up food from our plates and while he enthusiastically tried different flavours and textures he was still very reliant on my milk for sustenance and I was still happy to oblige. He began walking, and his first birthday came and went. Before I knew it I was breastfeeding a bright, active toddler. First he would use baby-signing to ask for milk, then later on he asked for 'boo-boo'. He was very sweet and he was still breastfeeding frequently day and night but I was happy with that. If we were busy, out shopping or at playgroup he wouldn't want to breastfeed unless tired or hurt. I found it was lovely to reconnect after a busy day and breastfeeding a toddler helped avoid many a meltdown. It was great to soothe a tired, fractious or frustrated little boy and it was an instant fix for colds, teething, bumps and grazes.

Sometime later that year, I reminded my husband of our earlier conversation and his feelings about breastfeeding an older baby. I observed that he didn't seem to have a problem with it now. He told me it just became a normal part of our lives. Our son was still only little and he could see how important the breastfeeding relationship was to him and how he was thriving on what we did, so to him it must be a 'good thing'.

Towards the end of my son's second year I fell pregnant. I researched a little on breastfeeding through pregnancy. I was healthy and had a straightforward pregnancy so there was no need to stop. I knew my milk production would dwindle and stop in order to make colostrum for the new baby at the end of pregnancy and that some children wean when the milk 'dries up' but my son continued. He got comfort from being close and suckling, and although it was uncomfortable at times I'm sure it helped with his transition to 'big brotherhood'. It was lovely to tandem feed and after the initial novelty of getting my milk supply back he went back to feeding only once or twice a day, usually just at bedtime.

If someone had told me before I had children that I would be a mum who breastfed their children through toddlerhood or beyond I would have thought them crazy. I didn't identify with my idea of the stereotypical 'hippy mum' at all and I still don't own a tie-dye maxi skirt! The transition from breastfeeding a little baby to feeding a strapping, active, walking, talking toddler/preschooler is so slow and gentle you almost don't notice. I consider myself fortunate in that I have been in a position to sustain our breastfeeding relationship as I realise it's not always possible or desirable. There seems to be a lot of pressure for mums to stop breastfeeding at some point and I've had doctors and other healthcare providers question me before, but I've been armed with information to share with and educate them.

Following my son's individual needs has helped me relax about issues some other mums stress about, such as picky eating or illness. My milk helps plug the gaps in their diet during fussy phases, keeps them hydrated when ill with a fever and is the quickest way to get them back to sleep after a bad dream or a noisy thunderstorm. Lots of people have misconceptions about longer term breastfeeding such as suggesting it keeps children dependent or makes them clingy. This hasn't been my experience, quite the opposite in fact. Breastfeeding through toddlerhood has been a very rewarding and positive experience for me and my children, and I wouldn't change it at all.

Chapter 11

AVOIDING difficult
situations

*When my kids become wild and unruly, I use a nice,
safe playpen. When they're finished I climb out.*

Erma Bombeck, American humourist

Have you ever been in a situation with your toddler that you wish you hadn't? It could be a stressful trip around a supermarket with a hungry, whining toddler or a playdate where your toddler and the host's toddler fought constantly, snatching toys from one another, pushing and shoving.

I can still vividly remember the worst day I ever had as a mother to toddlers. I was newly pregnant with violent morning sickness and ran a small craft business from home. I had run out of supplies and had a large order to fulfil. My son had been teething and we were both short on sleep from a disturbed night, but I needed to go to the craft shop. I buckled a reluctant toddler into his car seat and off we set. The craft shop was a toddler's paradise, so many different shapes, colours and textures, and as we entered the shop he made a beeline for the pen display, grabbing at the pens, eager to try them all, and with each one I prised from his fingers he found another replacement within seconds. Finally I managed to tear him away and we arrived at the scissor section; imagine the horror of your toddler lunging repeatedly at an assortment of sharp scissors glinting almost as much as the excitement in his eyes.

I couldn't take any more so I lifted him up and buckled him into the child seat in the shopping trolley; he was not amused at this at all and protested with loud screams. By now almost every customer in the shop was staring at me, at least that's what I felt; certainly in my imagination they were. My son proceeded to scream at the top of his lungs for the entire time we were in the shop, lunging at anything he could, pulling items off the shelf and kicking me in the stomach with his feet. I hurried to get my supplies as quickly as possible and, bright red with embarrassment, paid as quickly as I could. Back at the car I lifted my son up to put him in his car seat and in turn he arched into 'the back of steel' that so many toddlers possess when you are trying to fold them into a car seat. As I was trying to coax him to sit he kicked me square in the eye. I think it was more an accidental reflex than a kick on purpose, but it was the final straw for me. Anger overtook every cell in my being; I literally felt it rising like hot steam, from the pit of my stomach. I was too rough with the buckling in, I needed to scream, but I couldn't; I was in a public car park and people were looking at me, why were they looking at me? That made everything worse. I could only imagine what they were thinking. At that moment in time I felt like I hated everything; my son, myself, my husband for being at work and not having to deal with my son, my life in general, the people staring at us, you name it I hated it. Parenting was so hard; I wanted my old life back.

Somehow I managed to drive us home safely, my son screaming at the top of his lungs and kicking the back of my seat the whole way. I pulled up outside our house, and lifted him out of the seat in stony silence, with him pulling my hair. I carried him up to his cot, put him in, still wearing his coat and shoes, and walked out of his bedroom, slamming the door behind me. I went downstairs to the kitchen and sobbed my heart out for a good twenty minutes. The anger now had given way to guilt. I was the adult here, why had I been so mean to my son? What damage might I have caused him? I was an awful mother, the very worst in the world. I mopped my tears then climbed the stairs and headed back to his nursery. He was sleeping soundly; tear stains on his cheeks and his thick mop of curls damp with sweat and tears. I cried more; I felt like I cried all afternoon. I lifted him out of his cot and cradled him in my lap, still asleep and told him I was sorry, again and again and again. I told him I loved him and that next time I would be better, next time I wouldn't get angry, next time I wouldn't shout. Next time I would be the mummy he deserved and the mummy I so wanted to be.

That day still haunts me, and I am only grateful that he was too young to remember it. I have never felt such anger and regret in my life, particularly not within such a short space of time. I don't think people talk enough about the anger parents feel towards their children. If they did there would surely be more help and support?

Now I can look back, older and wiser, and think 'but why did I ever go out that day?' He was tired, I was tired and nauseous, and it was never going to end well. So, my craft order may have been late by a day or so, but in the grand scheme of things it really didn't matter. What mattered was looking after my son and looking after myself. The trip was never going to go smoothly; what was I thinking taking a toddler into a shop full of scissors? Why didn't I go at the weekend when my husband was home to take care of the toddler? It is so obvious to me now, but back then it really wasn't. It is just as I see so many situations between parents and toddlers now, and with an objective head I can think, 'Why didn't you just avoid the situation?' The truth is that when you're in the thick of things it can be so hard to take a step back and think objectively.

If there are certain situations where you really struggle with your toddler is it possible for you to avoid them? Do you really need to go? Do you really need to take them? Is there an alternative? Rescheduling, enlisting help or perhaps cancelling plans can sometimes save you both from enormous stress. Too many parents worry that avoiding situations in which there is conflict is the equivalent of 'giving in' and letting the toddler manipulate them. They worry about the escalating consequences of giving in, something often exacerbated by well-meaning relatives telling you, 'He's got to learn, you're too soft on him' or 'Don't let her win, you need to show her who's boss.' I didn't give in to my son in the situation I described above, but he most certainly didn't win; nobody did, we both lost and we both suffered. When toddlers experience huge, overwhelming emotions, just as my son did at the craft shop, they are never a 'winner'. Parenting is not a battle to be won; it is about balancing your needs with those of your child. If somebody is a winner that means that the other will be a loser, is that really what we want for our children? Avoiding situations that may trigger trauma is a wise strategy in achieving this balance.

You may think I am suggesting you just avoid any situation that you or your toddler find stressful. I am not; I am just suggesting that you might consider whether there are other options. Sometimes that might mean adapting your plans in some way, perhaps leaving a playdate early if your toddler is overwhelmed, taking a friend to the shops with you for mutual support or rescheduling your day so that you time your plans with your toddler's naps. Many toddlers struggle with playdates at their own homes, particularly when we make them share their toys with their toddler friends. One good way to avoid this trauma is to pack up your child's toys and have a special few toys that are for playdates only. That way you can avoid your toddler's protestations at sharing his prized possessions. If your toddler still finds the playdate stressful don't be afraid to ask your visitors to leave; far from being rude, what you are really showing is your concern for your toddler. One of the keys to calmer toddler parenting is all about being flexible and responsive to your child.

HOW TO COPE WHEN YOUR TODDLER IS HAVING A TANTRUM

- Firstly make sure your toddler is safe and cannot harm anyone else; if not try to find a safe space nearby. If your toddler is kicking, hitting or biting you remind him that it's OK to be angry and feel the need to kick/hit/bite but it's not OK to do it to you because it hurts, and offer him a safe acceptable alternative instead.

- Next take a few seconds to regulate your own emotions. Take a few deep breaths and remind yourself that your toddler is 'having a hard time' not 'giving you a hard time' and as the adult it is your job to help your toddler to feel safe, respected and heard in order that they may learn the skill of emotional self-regulation when they are older. Do this for as long as you need to in order to respond calmly to your toddler.

- Try to ignore any onlookers, remembering your long-term parenting goals and taking comfort in them, knowing that you are doing your best for your toddler and focusing on their long-term personality as well as the short term.

- Let your toddler know you are there for them if and when they want you. Just a simple, 'Mummy is here if you would like a hug' is enough.

- Name the emotions your toddler is experiencing and use the 'say what you see' approach to validate your toddler's feelings: 'I can see you are very sad that I didn't buy you the toy, you really wanted it didn't you? It made you really angry when I said no. I'm sorry.'

- Remind your toddler again that you are there for them: 'When you're ready let me know and we can have a cuddle and I can help you to calm down.'

- When your toddler decides to come to you give him a big hug and tell him how much you love him. Remind him that it's OK to be angry and sad.

- When the tantrum is over remember it is just that – over. It's time to continue with your day, leaving the tantrum and any feelings it evoked in you in the past.

Avoiding negative parenting comments

As well as avoiding situations that are stressful for your toddler it may also be worth considering avoiding situations that you find stressful. I don't think there is any more stressful situation to find yourself in as a fairly new parent than one where you are in the company of a 'parenting know it all', particularly if that person has very different ideas to you about parenting. For many parents time spent in the presence of friends, and more likely relatives, quick to criticise their parenting choices and offer their own advice on how to get little Johnny to 'sleep through the night' and 'stop being so clingy' is perhaps more stressful than enduring any behaviour your toddler can come up with.

Why do you think others feel it is their place to criticise our parenting choices? I think for a large majority there is no underlying malicious cause, but in many cases I think it is because our nearest and dearest struggle to understand why we make life so hard for ourselves. They see that we are tired, they see a toddler who is only happy when in physical contact with us, they see a toddler whom they think they needs to stop manipulating you and they see a toddler whose eating habits concern them. In most cases they want to try to help, as they don't think it is right that we are making such martyrs of ourselves when we're obviously so tired and in need of a break. They don't really think deeper than this when they suggest, 'He needs a good old smack, it never did my children any harm.' In the majority of cases, while these comments might deeply upset us and feel like a slant on our own parenting choices, and indeed our children, I do believe that in many cases they are only said out of genuine concern and compassion.

The next point to bear in mind is that the approach I have discussed in this book is not 'the done thing' in our society. The television programmes your friends and relatives watch, and the books, magazines and newspaper articles that they read paint a very different picture of toddlers and the related discipline of them. With this in mind it is no surprise that they might struggle to understand the 'strange' choices you are making, which frankly don't fit with anything they know. Sometimes when we struggle to understand something we can come across as hostile

and closed minded, when we're just feeling confused and insecure that our beliefs are being challenged.

If you receive comments that upset you, perhaps from your
own parents or your in-laws, remember that the way we parent
probably isn't the same as the way we were parented. Imagine
how it might feel for your own parents to see you parenting in
a different way; as well as not understanding the choices that you
are making, your parenting may also invoke guilt in them,
sorrow for what they didn't know and potentially even anger at
the choices you are making that are deliberately different to the
way they parented you. Your choices might even cause your parents or in-laws to question if they were good enough parents
themselves. Imagine how hard it must be to see a younger generation parenting in a completely different way to the way you
parented; in many ways it must seem like a slur on your choices.
Sometimes such thoughts can bring up long-buried guilt and
sorrow. Some parents and in-laws can be wonderfully accepting
and may be able to forgive themselves and accept your choices
with open arms, but for others the amount of self-reflection and
forgiveness they have to process can be just too huge. The cognitive dissonance they experience must be overwhelming, so
perhaps it is easier to attack your choices than be critical of their
own.

Tips for coping with parenting criticism

1. Remember the respect and empathy that you aim to
   show to your child; why not try to use the same respect
   and empathy to relate to the difficult relatives? Just as I
   always say that no child is inherently 'bad', I really
   don't believe any adult is inherently bad either. There
   is always a reason for their behaviour. You don't have

to understand the reason, or even know why, just knowing there is one is enough. Your parenting has sparked an uncomfortable feeling in your friend or relative, so remembering that it is not about you, but it is about them, can make the world of difference to your reaction.

2. Don't take the comments personally. Their comments aren't really about you and your child; they are about their own childhood, their own experience of parenting, their peer pressure, the books they read as a new parent, their relatives, their lack of awareness of modern day science. Remember, too, that they might not be open to being re-educated, even though it would make things infinitely easier for you. You could try this approach: 'I hear what you're saying, Mum, and I really respect your opinion. I wonder if you know that there has been quite a lot of research into this in the last few years. The information I have now is very different to the information you had when you had me. I'd love to talk to you about it someday, or I have a great book I could lend you if you'd like to read what I've read?' Above all though, know that you are making the right choices for your family with the information you have right now; don't let their comments dent your confidence!

3. If it's obvious that they don't want to hear what you have to say then sometimes it is easier for everyone if, first, you try to avoid the conversations and, second, try to limit the discussions as much as possible. Avoidance of these conversations is often the easiest way. For instance, the next time you hear, 'I don't know why you won't give him a clip round the ear,' you could try smiling and saying, 'You know I really value your opinion, but we feel this is the right way for us at the moment,' rather than being pulled into a lengthy discussion.

4. Similarly, on the avoidance theme once more, try deflecting their attention. If they are telling you that you child needs a good dose of discipline, try responding with something like, 'Oh wow, you have new earrings. They are lovely, where did you get them from?' Hopefully this will give them the message that you don't wish to discuss the issue any more.

This chapter has been possibly the hardest for me to write, as it has brought up so many old memories of my time with my own toddlers. With the benefit of hindsight there is so much I would love to go back and change if I could, and in particular there are certain situations that I really wish I had made the decision to avoid. This is the story of one of them.

My story

When my little boy, Seb, turned a year old we started visiting a local playgroup. While I loved staying at home with him and pottering around doing our own thing, I have to be honest and say I hated going to playgroup each week. My son was really not interested in playing with the other children; he only wanted to be with me. Each time we went I would try to encourage him to play with the other children, but the more I encouraged him the more he clung to me and the more I worried about how shy and antisocial he was. He did enjoy the messy play, such as painting and gluing, but this wasn't anything that we didn't already do at home. Almost every week that we went there would be a fight over toys and, as Seb was quite passive, he would usually let the other child take the toy and end up in my lap in floods of tears. On several occasions the disagreements became physical and he was usually on the receiving end, though not always, and there were several occasions when I found myself apologising for his behaviour to other parents and carers.

Towards the end of each session the helpers used to gather all of the children together and seat them around little tables, and they then brought out juice in small, plastic, open-topped cups and a plate of assorted biscuits; this was a huge cause of stress to Seb and me each week. Firstly he hadn't yet mastered the art of drinking out of an open-topped cup, so inevitably each week he would knock his juice over, and each week I would feel more embarrassed and angrier at him. I would watch the other children drinking nicely out of their open-top cups with ease. They didn't spill theirs; why was it always me apologising for my son? Why couldn't he drink like them? The biscuit plate was also another huge source of stress for both of us as there was only one certain type of bis-cuit on it that he liked. If the plate started off at our end of the table things were peaceful as Seb would generally get the bis-cuit that he liked, but if it started off at the other end of the table, meaning the only biscuit he liked had already been taken, things were a different matter and a tantrum inevitably ensued.

After the trauma of snack time we would form a circle for 'song time'. I cannot tell you how much I hated song time. Ten years on and I still feel a knot of nausea forming in my stom-ach whenever I hear the songs 'Dingle Dangle Scarecrow' or 'Sleeping Bunnies'. Neither of us enjoyed singing in public and this was obviously clear to the play leaders who used to try enthusiastically to get us both to join in, much to my dismay and Seb's disgust.

After almost a year of enduring weekly visits, most of which followed the above pattern, I used to dread playgroup days; in fact the dread started the night before. I told myself, however, that it was important to keep going, for Seb's sake, as it was important that he socialised with other children and learnt to share. Finally, though, I realised that our visits were stressful for both of us, that Seb disliked it as much as I did and would be guaranteed to cry over something every week. What he really wanted was to be with me, pottering around the house or garden, visiting the local shops or feeding ducks. I think I just didn't have the confidence to trust that I was enough for him at the beginning. Going to playgroup was 'the done thing' and so I followed suit, and in the beginning I never considered not going, why would I? All of my friends went; surely I would be a bad mother if I didn't take him?

Once I really understood Seb's needs, though, I realised that playgroup was not the right place for him, or for me; it was a place that stressed us both every week. After this realisation and the new confidence I had gained to know that I was enough for him, I cancelled his place and we never looked back, we were both happier. Seb drank happily from a closed-top cup for another two years and always had his favourite biscuits at home, I stocked up on paints and glue and we sang to the radio at home, often dancing too. He didn't need playgroup, he just needed me. I just wish I had realised that sooner, as if I had it would have spared us both a lot of trauma.

Chapter 12

The importance of unconditional LOVE

What a child doesn't receive he can seldom later give.

P. D. James, author

'm sure many people will wonder, 'Why has she included a whole chapter about loving our children in her book?' After all, we all love our toddlers don't we? The type of love I would like to talk about in this chapter, however, is unconditional love, that is love that does not depend on whether your toddler is 'naughty' or 'good'. It doesn't depend on them sitting and playing nicely rather than tantruming loudly, it is love that is ever present, whatever your toddler is or isn't doing. Of course we always love our children, even though sometimes we may not like them very much, but do we always show our children this love? Or is our display of love conditional upon their behaviour?

Love withdrawal techniques

Think about the messages toddlers might receive when they are sent to 'time out', put on the naughty step or sent to their room; some psychologists call these punishments 'love withdrawal techniques'. We know from neuropsychology that a two- or three-year-old does not have the brain development necessary to understand fully why you have withdrawn your love for them (for this is how they will see it, even if you do not) and nor are they capable of thinking rationally about their behaviour or their future actions. To a toddler placed in 'time out' we withdraw our love and support at a time when they need it the most. We know that toddlers have big feelings that they cannot control, we know that tantrums are as scary to a toddler as they are irritating to us; we know that toddlers need our help to diffuse their big emotions and to feel safe, they need our love all of the time and they need it unconditionally. In fact the times when a toddler is at his least lovable are often the times when he needs your love the most.

Why toddlers need our love

Back in 1951, psychologist John Bowlby, the founding father of attachment theory, wrote a publication for the World Health Organisation, where he stated, 'The infant and young child should experience a warm, intimate, and continuous relationship with his mother (or permanent mother substitute) in which both find satisfaction and enjoyment and that not to do so may have significant and irreversible mental health consequences.' Research into children separated from their parents during and after the Second World War and those hospitalised without their parents' presence showed psychologists just how vital love was to the healthy development of the child. Without this love and proximity of their parents the children did not thrive. Love is as important to a child as water, food and air. It is a need that all children need fulfilling, which is as real as any other physical need.

This idea can be summed up neatly by looking at the work of American psychologist Abraham Maslow, who is famed for the invention of what he calls the 'hierarchy of needs', a simple representation of the needs of human beings in order for them to not only survive, but to thrive and reach their full potential in life. I like to use Maslow's principles and ideas to think about what he might have created if he had designed a Hierarchy of Needs specifically for toddlers. I think it would look something like this:

The ToddlerCalm™ toddler's hierarchy of needs

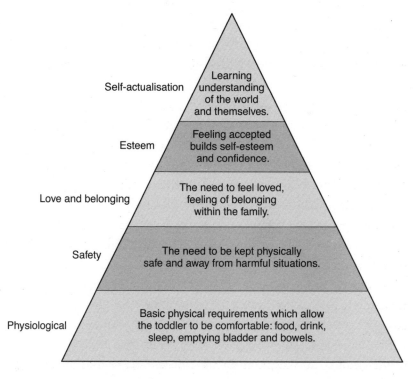

* Based on the work of Abraham Maslow and his 'hierarchy of needs' (1943)

Working up from the base of the pyramid (the lowest layer being the most basic needs of a toddler), we see that it is important that a strong foundation is built in order for the other levels to build upon one another. Each foundation level must be strong enough for the toddler to reach the next level, and so on. If one level is weak for a child, then the needs above that level will be very difficult to develop, if not impossible, because all of the needs interrelate. The pyramid shows us that if a toddler does not feel loved, unconditionally, self-esteem, confidence and a passion for learning about the world in which we live will be traits that the child is very unlikely to develop. Put simply, if a toddler is not loved unconditionally they cannot reach the peak of their abilities.

The hormone of love

Research shows us that the release of oxytocin (the hormone of love) aids empathy, which means that the more we shower our toddlers with love, the greater the bond and relationship and the more we are able to understand our toddlers, and in turn they are more likely to grow to be empathic adults themselves. As Kerstin Uvnäs Moberg, author of *The Oxytocin Factor*, says, 'We may end up in a society where we have weakened the oxytocin system. That might mean that people become less interactive, less friendly and more stressed.' Oxytocin is secreted when we feel loved, when we hug and when we have skin to skin contact with one another.

Research[30] undertaken in 2007 highlights the importance of raising a child in a loving environment, rich in oxytocin. Scientists found that after giving healthy male volunteers an oxytocin supplement they were more able to 'read the minds' of other people. As I have said before, I do not mean mind reading in a spiritual sense, rather reading another's feelings through their faces, or as we might say – empathy. If oxytocin can make us more empathic, then surely toddlers who have rich supplies of this love hormone during the critical early years of life will be more likely to grow to be empathic, kind and understanding adults?

The smart phone and the 'still face'

More and more of us own smart phones and laptops. They have become a vital part of our lives and something we simply cannot live without. How often are you busy writing an email or sending a text message when your toddler asks you something? How often do you put your telephone or laptop down, look them in the eye and respond? Or do you carry on looking at the screen, saying, 'Hmmm, just a minute, darling'? I know I do the latter far too often.

What are we conveying to our toddlers with this lack of eye contact and attention?

In the late 1970s psychologist Edward Tronick and his fellow researchers introduced us to the idea of the 'still face' experiment. Put simply this experiment showed the importance of facial and eye contact and responsiveness from parent to child. During the experiment, which now has many guises, parents were told to keep their face still and 'mask like' and unresponsive to their infants, who very quickly get incredibly distressed. To the child mummy and daddy might be there in person, but their unresponsiveness shows that they are not really available for the child. A quick internet search will show you many video clips of the experiments, which are very disturbing. I can't help thinking about the similarities between this experiment and the faces we present to our children while using smart phones and the like and I fear this will only increase the more technology takes over our lives.

Obviously the message from this is to try to use our laptops and smart phones less around our children, though some would just say use them less, full stop! A good tactic that I like to suggest too is that if your toddler asks for your attention, instead of the usual response of 'Wait just a minute, darling', try to stop what you are doing and say, 'I am really busy right now, but I can give you my attention for a minute' there and then, rather than making your toddler wait for what is inevitably a lot longer than 'just a minute'. The results of using this tactic can be astounding, so why not try it and see?

Containing your toddler's uncomfortable feelings

Why would we respond to a toddler tantrum with compassion rather than punishment? This is certainly not the 'done thing' in society, is it? The usual suggestion is that parents need to teach their toddler a lesson and nip the bad behaviour in the bud so that the toddler learns he is not the one in control and can't have everything he wants, when he wants it. Think about how confusing and scary a tantrum is for a toddler though, and imagine that the toddler's wails and whines are really a call for help, your toddler's way of saying, 'These feelings are too big for me, I can't cope, please help me.' As a parent you have a choice of responding in two different ways: one of these validates the toddler's feelings with unconditional love and helps them to diffuse their feelings; the other reflects the feelings straight back to the toddler, sometimes amplified. When you ignore or punish a tantrum the toddler has no opportunity to diffuse their feelings, as the very person they need to help them to cope and teach them how to regulate their emotions has become unavailable to them, compounding the issue even more.

If we are able to contain our toddler's unsettling feelings, we enable them to release emotions that may otherwise build inside them, which could manifest as more worrying behaviour later in life. By containing their big emotions we also help our toddlers to trust us, to know that we do indeed love them unconditionally and will always be there for them. By containing our toddlers' scary feelings we show them that we respect them and in turn this helps them to respect us, which means that they are more likely to listen to us and respond to our requests when we ask them to please do something for us, they will be intrinsically motivated to help us out of love and respect. If we are compassionate towards our toddlers they will mirror back this positive behaviour to us.

I find the best way to explain this process, referred to by psychologists as 'containment', is pictorially, as in the example overleaf.

The importance of loving ourselves

Containing our toddler's big emotions is hard work and if we are in need of containment ourselves it will be almost impossible. What do I mean by this? I mean if you are full of stress and worry, if you do not take care of your needs and nurture yourself and if you have no way of emptying your own big feelings it will be impossible for you to take on board those of your child.

Just as with any container, our own containers do not hold infinite quantities; there will always be a time when our container will be 'full up'. In our modern day world of parenting, with such little support it is very easy to get 'full up' ourselves. We no longer have the close knit family and 'village' style support that our ancestors had, we have to juggle the demands of parenting with our professional lives, we have mortgages and bills to pay and the ever increasing expectations of society to be

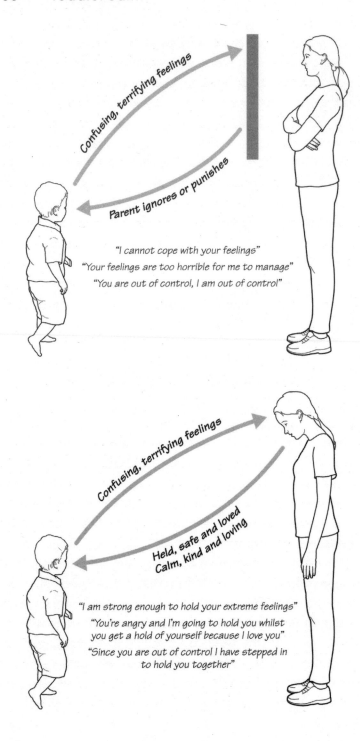

Confusing, terrifying feelings

Parent ignores or punishes

"I cannot cope with your feelings"
"Your feelings are too horrible for me to manage"
"You are out of control, I am out of control"

Confusing, terrifying feelings

Held, safe and loved
Calm, kind and loving

"I am strong enough to hold your extreme feelings"

"You're angry and I'm going to hold you whilst
you get a hold of yourself because I love you"

"Since you are out of control I have stepped in
to hold you together"

'yummy mummies'. Something has to give. If we cannot find a way to offload our own worries and concerns, if we cannot find a way to love and respect ourselves and nurture our own needs, it will be almost impossible for our containers to be empty enough to take on board our toddlers' big emotions.

Indeed, this could be one of the biggest challenges faced by parents, when our lives are so busy, we run ourselves into the ground and it's no surprise that we find it hard to be the parents we want to be, but in almost all cases though **you** are the key. **You** are the key for calming your toddler, **you** are the key for stopping their unwanted behaviour, **you** are the key for helping your child to grow up to be a calm, kind and empathic individual; there are no short-cut miracle fixes in parenting, and that's a big deal. I know when I first realised that, I felt a huge responsibility and burden, to know that ultimately I was responsible for my child's behaviour and I alone (well, myself and my husband) had the power to solve our own dilemmas. Too many parents try to fix their toddlers when it is perhaps themselves they need to fix.

You must realise how important you are, that you need a container too, you need somebody to offload your own concerns to and you need somebody to help you to take care of your own needs. If you are lucky enough to have friends and family nearby do not be afraid to ask for help; if you do not have friends and family nearby there are plenty or organisations who can help. I have listed them at the back of this book; some offer their services free of charge, some you may have to pay for.

Many parents are so concerned about taking care of their children they forget how to take care of themselves. What do you do for yourself? How do you show yourself unconditional love? I strongly believe that self-love is perhaps the most important love of all and that too many parents neglect their own needs in the quest for fulfilling every need of their child's, but very often their selflessness backfires and by neglecting their own needs they find that, ultimately, everyone is left in need. This is something I have had to take stock of lately and make provisions to change, as like most parents I had neglected self-love for far too long.

Learning to nurture ourselves as a parent

Many years ago, long before I had children, I used to be an artist. Indeed that's how I was known to most people as a teenager: 'Sarah – the one who's brilliant at art.' I won every art competition I entered; I went to private school on an art scholarship and had dreams of attending Goldsmiths College to study Fine Art one day. Somewhere along the way I lost that piece of myself, my paints cracked and dried up, my portfolio case was resigned to the attic and the only time I ever picked up a paintbrush was to paint a mural on my baby son's nursery walls. My identity was now 'Sarah the mum'. I absolutely didn't mind that, it was the best identity ever, but the need to reclaim that part of me I lost grew every day. I felt the need to be completely 'me' again, some might say I felt the need to be selfish, but I needed to be more than just 'all things parenting'. I needed to be 'Sarah' again, so I enrolled in art classes and spent the money I would ordinarily spend on my children on new art equipment for myself. I converted our run-down old study to an art studio, with the idea that it would be my sanctuary, my retreat when things got too much. You might think that this is unrelated to parenting, but it isn't, it is central to my parenting, it is how I recharge and unwind, ready to take on a brand new day and all of the parenting challenges I will face.

When I'm tired and stressed, working to deadlines and making myself too available for other people, I invest no energy into myself, body and soul. I neglect to nourish my body with healthy food and I neglect to feed my mind with any of my passions. When I'm stressed I am 'snappy, shouty mum', irritable, grumpy and hyper-critical. If I'm all wrung out I have nothing to give, to myself and especially not to others. For me to be the best mother I can be I need to spend time away from my children, I need time to nurture myself. How can I possibly nurture anyone else if I am in dire need of soul food myself?

I learnt this lesson the hard way in my early days working as a doula (birth companion) and I recount the story time and again to parents I meet. It was my first doula job, I was super-keen. I had packed an enormous bag full of 'stuff' I thought that the labouring mum might need. I was ready to give my job and the birthing family my all. I arrived in the late afternoon and skipped dinner that evening; I was on an adrenaline high and didn't need the food. We stayed awake all night while the mother laboured. I didn't dare go to sleep (How could I sleep? I was being paid to look after her. It would surely be rude for me to snooze?), I didn't eat breakfast either, you see I hadn't packed anything for myself in my giant bag, as I felt that I didn't really matter on this momentous day. Lunchtime rolled round (it was a long labour), another meal missed and only one glass of water was consumed in what was getting on for twenty hours. It was summer, it was hot and stuffy, and I felt like I could barely breathe. Just as the mother entered her birthing pool, nearing the end of her labour, my head started to spin. 'Oh my goodness I'm going to faint,' I thought and not wanting to cause a drama I rushed out of the room, I gulped down a pint of fresh orange juice and stood outside in the garden, gasping the cool air for as long as I dared be away. I returned moments before the baby was born. I had not been there at the time the mother needed me the most. In my quest to 'always be there for her' I had neglected my own needs and in doing so I had failed to give my support when she really needed me.

What lesson did I learn? In my later doula births I put myself first. That might sound wrong and not very 'doula like', but I think it was my most powerful lesson. My doula bag dramatically shrank in size and became all about me; I packed it full of drinks, food and comfort items for me and barely anything for the women in labour. I learnt that if I didn't look after myself I couldn't possibly look after others. I learnt that I mattered; I learnt that I must start with nurturing myself before I could think about anybody else and I became a much better doula for it.

As a busy, working, stay at home mum to four young children, with no childcare or domestic help, I need to put myself first. I matter. If I don't look after myself who will? If I don't look after myself how can I be there for my children? Again this was a lesson learnt late in my parenting journey but one I cannot stress enough to any parents. Look after your own needs, nurture yourself; feed your body, your soul and your mind. Do what you need to do to be calm and relaxed. Find a hobby, go swimming, go to yoga classes, take up running, book a massage or take long, thoughtful walks. Find somebody that you can talk to, to offload your own concerns or perhaps write a diary. I have monthly reflexology sessions, many long relaxing baths with indulgent bubble bath and my art studio, when I can; I try to spend a day at a spa with girlfriends too. I also find blogging incredibly cathartic, and writing for me is my support network, I offload my worries and stress into my laptop. I don't have any close family, aside from my husband, as I lost both of my parents when I was in my early twenties and have no siblings, so I need to seek my support elsewhere.

If there is one thing that you can do to change your parenting and the behaviour of your toddler I really believe it is this. When you are nurtured yourself, everything is easier, and because you are calmer your children naturally will be too. It is an ever perpetuating circle, which can either work very positively or end very badly.

So, with all of that in mind, how will you nurture yourself today? How will you empty your 'container' so that you have the space necessary to give to your toddler?

Mother substitutes
and separation anxiety

Many parents worry that they love their children too much (I promise you that this is impossible) and that in turn their toddler may become clingy and needy. We are often advised that our toddlers 'need to learn to cope on their own' and we should encourage separation from us in order to encourage their independence. One of the best measures of 'secure attachment', however, is a young child who is comfortable to explore the world in the presence of his parents and very upset when his mother or father leaves. The only problem is that in our culture this is not seen as normal, it is seen as undesirable and an example of 'clingy' behaviour, and in many cases it is seen as a failing on the part of the parents to 'detach' and grow a confident child. This couldn't be further from the truth, as is the incorrect assumption made by society that 'in order to create a confident independent child we must push them out into the world so they can learn we are not always there'.

True independence is not learnt through rewards, punishments and force, but from a loving, secure relationship with caregivers at a young age. If your toddler is not happy for you to leave them anywhere therefore, rather than being a cause for concern that you've done something wrong and will have a shy, clingy child living with you until their thirties, actually his 'clingy' behaviour could be interpreted as a way of him congratulating you.

This is all well and good, but I do understand that sometimes you need to leave your toddler, perhaps you need to work, and perhaps you just need a day or a weekend to yourself to empty your containment jar in order to make you a better container for your toddler. Here it is a good idea to consider using what psychologists refer to as a 'mother substitute', whether that is a kind, empathic caregiver such as a child-minder, nanny or another member of your family who agrees with your parenting ethos. You could also consider finding a material object to help your child to ease into the transition of separation as smoothly as possible; unsurprisingly psychologists call these objects 'transitional objects'.

Paediatrician and psychoanalyst Donald Winnicott has spoken widely about 'transitional objects' or 'comfort objects'. Such objects can be teddy bears, dummies, blankets or 'lovies', or any other object a toddler can use to transition from complete dependence to relative independence from you. Helping your toddler to feel as 'close' to you as possible through an object they closely associate with you can help them hugely during times when you need to be away from them. Some parents give their toddler an item of their clothing to hug, a muslin cloth spritzed with their perfume or even a photograph of themselves to carry around. Some even record their voices, talking to their little one or singing a lullaby. Just make sure you have more than one of these objects; I speak from experience when I tell you how awful it is when a toddler loses their favourite comforter.

WHAT IS THE BEST WAY TO LEAVE YOUR TODDLER WHEN YOU REALLY HAVE TO?

- Preparation really is the key for times when leaving your toddler is unavoidable. Ideally, before you leave your toddler try to ensure that he has a strong bond with the person who will be looking after him. If you are leaving your toddler at nursery, for instance, then attend with him a good few times while he gets to know his new caregiver. It is a good idea to take a photograph of your toddler and his new caregiver and refer to them regularly at home with the photograph and talking about how much fun your toddler and his new caregiver have together and how you're looking forward to everyone playing together again soon.

- Use a transitional object if your child has one; if not think about using one well in advance of when the separation needs to take place.

- When you first have to leave your toddler, try to do it for a short period of time, for instance thirty minutes or an hour, slowly build on this a little at a time if you can.

- When you leave ensure you always say goodbye and never sneak out. No matter what others may suggest it is important for your toddler to know when you have gone and by sneaking out you may confuse and upset them even more.

- Keep your goodbyes as cheery and positive as possible, however you may be feeling yourself, and reassure your toddler you will be back soon. Try to make sure your toddler is with their caregiver when you leave so that the caregiver can comfort them quickly.

- Invent a 'goodbye routine', for instance the words you use to say goodbye and kissing first your toddler's teddy bear, then your toddler and the teddy bear again or perhaps you could even make up your own song? The ritual will help your toddler to know that this means that you will be leaving soon and should also help to reassure him that you will always come back.

- Try to resist the temptation to hang around outside and listen to your toddler crying; it doesn't help anyone, least of all you, if you really have to leave him.

Surviving separation anxiety

Related to the above point of self-love, if your toddler is having trouble separating from you then you need to be kind to yourself. This is the real key to surviving these tricky periods. You can't do much to speed your toddler through this stage, nor can you stop them from feeling totally normal feelings, but what you can do is to change how you respond. In order to respond with compassion for your toddler you need to nurture yourself. Sleep when you can, enlist help from people your toddler already has a secure attachment with, even if it is just for them to sit playing with your toddler for an hour while you soak in the bath, ask people to prepare meals for you, and consider temporarily employing a cleaner or somebody to do your washing and ironing for you (try your local launderette's service wash). Find something that helps you to relax mentally – yoga, relaxation CDs, running, reading a good book and know that 'this too will pass'.

The easiest way to survive separation anxiety is with the help of your family and friends, this is the key – as summed up so well by the father of attachment theory, John Bowlby, himself: 'Just as children are absolutely dependent on their parents for sustenance, so in all but the most primitive communities, are parents, especially their mothers, dependent on a greater society for economic provision. If a community values its children it must cherish their parents.'

Indeed I think this is the best way to survive parenting full stop; enlist as much help and support from others as you possibly can.

Louise's story

I don't think any parent means to love their child conditionally. I'm sure my parents didn't. But when it comes to relationships, what matters most is not your intention, but what the other person feels. When my mother said, 'I love you but I don't like you at the moment' – what she meant was 'I love you but I'm not comfortable with your behaviour.' What I felt as a child was, 'You're not a nice person; I only love you because I have to.'

What we have to remember as parents is that we are the most influential and highly regarded people in our children's lives. If we say or imply we don't like something (including the child), they will believe us, and ultimately take on that belief themselves. Through comments such as the one above, as well as things like 'Why can't you be like your sister?', along with constant ridiculing, teasing and snide comments about things that didn't please my mother, the belief I came to hold about myself was 'I'm not a nice/good/lovable person, and when people get to know the real me, they won't like me either'. As an adult I find it hard to have close friends, preferring many friends that I keep at a distance, for fear they might not like me if they know me well. Not that I blame my parents. I know they were only repeating what they were shown, and so the cycle continues . . .

I am a very emotional person and cry easily. Another vivid memory is the rejection of my tears as a child, and even as a young adult. I know now that this was because my tears invoked guilt and uncomfortable feelings in my parents. However, rather than admit this (to themselves or me), they would either ridicule me or dismiss my tears or, worst of all, imply I was crying to 'get my own way' or 'get some sympathy' or 'manipulate the situation'. The feeling of absolute despair that I couldn't even release my hurt through crying, through fear of being judged or labelled, was one of the worst. Needless to say once I started crying – which was often and quickly in any row – I was no longer taken seriously or listened to. I was usually sent away at that point. Rejected, pushed away, 'get out of my sight and I don't want to see you again until you sort yourself out'.

Unfortunately my parents' love was so conditional, it came to be how we loved them too. After all, we only had their model to go on. My three sisters and I were estranged from our father for a few years in our teens, and have now been estranged from our mother for ten years. They taught us (without intending to) that if someone behaves in a way that you disagree with, you don't love them any more. Even if they are your closest family where there are supposed to be stronger ties. I used to worry sometimes that I'm incapable of unconditional love. But as soon as I had my daughter I knew it wasn't true, and while it made me understand my own mother's actions even less, it made me determined to be the one to break this cycle of conditional love so powerful as it has escalated through the generations that it has ultimately led to the complete destruction of my family. So while the situation is sad, and was extremely painful at the time, I am in a strange way grateful for the intensity of it, as perhaps I wouldn't have questioned how I was parented if it didn't lead to such an extreme result.

Saying all this, as much as I get the theory, and can wax lyrical to anyone who'll listen about choices I've made, I sometimes find it hard to maintain my ideals. In the heat of the moment I often find myself saying or doing things I'm not happy with (none of us are perfect after all). However, I try to reflect on everything, correct anything immediately that I'm uncomfortable with, and talk through things and listen with understanding ears in a bid to save the next generation. I also try to reflect on the good things too, to take pride when I'm pleased with my handling of a situation, and encouragement from the knowledge that through this reflection and insight into myself, over time I will edge closer to where I want to be, which is a place where my daughter knows I love her, unconditionally and for ever.

Chapter 13

Why you don't need to be permissive to parent respectfully

The child supplies the power but the parents have to do the steering.

Dr Benjamin Spock, author and childcare expert

Quite often I receive emails from anxious parents who have read articles I have written and become worried that I suggest they should never say 'no' to their toddler for fear of upsetting them or making them cry. This is not what I am saying: I believe truly respectful parenting needs to be mindful of not only the toddler's safety, but also of our long-term parenting goals. Our toddlers need our help to reach these goals, just as they need our help to understand the rules of society, to understand what is and what isn't acceptable behaviour, that they cannot always have or do what they want, when they want, and they need our help to understand the consequences of their actions.

To be truly respectful and empathic towards our toddlers we need to also think about our long-term goals for them, the goals that I asked you to think about in chapter 1, as well as the short term. Sometimes we can be so afraid of upsetting our toddler that we do not say 'no' enough. Just because you may say 'no' to your toddler, whether they might want an ice cream for breakfast, or an expensive toy they see on a shopping trip, it does not make you unempathic or disrespectful. It is quite the opposite in fact, for you are helping your toddler to learn important life lessons. If you punished them, perhaps with 'time out' or ignoring them, when the inevitable tears or tantrums ensued, this indeed would indicate a lack of understanding and compassion towards them. Helping them to understand, name and express their uncomfortable emotions, however, and 'sitting with' them (both in a physical and emotional sense) while they express their emotions is perhaps the most compassionate thing you can do as a parent.

The permissive parenting myth

It is a commonly held misconception that those who parent their babies and children with respect and compassion are permissive parents. The assumption here is that in trying to afford their children respect and empathy these parents allow their offspring always to get their own way, thus creating future selfish, 'me, me' and 'I want it all **now**' adults. Sometimes society calls this 'permissive parenting', sometimes it is called 'pandering to children', sometimes it is called 'allowing our children to manipulate us', but whatever words are used it all comes back down to the same misunderstanding.

Similarly, many parents who follow their heart and their instincts, but not the experts' rigid rules and routines commonly used to parent toddlers, are accused of 'parenting by accident'. It is suggested that they are too soft on their children, not really thinking things through or planning for the future, and in doing so they are creating huge problems in their wake, usually in the shape of raising a selfish, needy child.

What is really being voiced here is a misunderstanding of infant psychology and the long-term effects that these authoritarian methods of parenting can produce. Why do we consider children to be such an inconvenience and why do we tend to view their normal behaviour as anything but and try to fix problems that don't really exist in order to have an easier life as parents? When did our culture become so 'childist'?

That isn't to say that some parents do merit a 'permissive parenting' label, for I have met many parents I would consider to be permissive. There are those who do not enforce boundaries and limits on their toddler's behaviour and those who seemingly allow their toddler to do whatever they want. Often these parents are concerned that their child should never cry because of their, the parents', actions but instead believe that they should always be left 'to experiment' and to 'express their freedom' and there are those who are reluctant to discipline their toddlers at all.

Compassionate, respectful parenting is mindful always of the importance of attachment and the parent–infant dyad, however, it never prescribes that parents should always let the child get their own way, and never suggests that children shouldn't be set firm boundaries. In fact, in reality it is quite the opposite. Respectful parenting focuses on understanding and responding to a child's needs and sometimes, often in fact, the child needs steering to help them to understand the demands and expectations of society, and to develop an understanding of social rules. This means that we need to set firm boundaries and limits for our children and very often our children will not like our requests, often showing their distaste through their tantrums and tears.

Take, for instance, the example of a naturally curious two-year-old forming a schema about the properties of liquids. Imagine that the little bundle of exploration finds a bottle of expensive shampoo on the side of the bath. Our little scientist realises that the flip top lid allows him to open the lid easily and the soft bottle allows for easy squeezing, so he promptly squeezes the whole of the contents onto the bathroom floor. Imagine the toddler being enthralled by the shiny, glossy, thick liquid coming out of the bottle and making patterns on the floor, over the bath towel and the bath mat. Imagine then the toddler wondering how fantastic it would be to use your new toothbrush to move the liquid on the bathroom floor around into new patterns. In this example the little boy is not 'being naughty', he is just exploring his world with a sense of curious wonder and he would be learning more about the properties of liquids than in any science lesson. It is certainly a great learning and creative experience for him, but the expensive shampoo has now all gone, the new toothbrush is ruined, a new load of washing is created and you have a good hour of cleaning to do in the bathroom. I don't know about you but this isn't the sort of behaviour I would like to encourage in my toddlers.

Faced with a situation such as this a permissive parent would probably allow the toddler to carry on, reluctant to apprehend, knowing that if they take the shampoo and toothbrush away then the toddler would probably cry and most likely escalate to a full-on tantrum very quickly. The permissive parent therefore might resign themselves to the mess, the financial cost and the cost in time it would take for them to clear up the mess when the toddler became bored. I believe that this is not an example of true compassionate parenting. Faced with this situation a truly compassionate parent would take the shampoo and toothbrush from the toddler (after all expensive shampoo and a brand new toothbrush are really not appropriate toddler playthings), empathise with the toddler that although this looks like great fun unfortunately it is not acceptable. The parent would calmly explain why the toddler could not play with the shampoo and toothbrush, and offer them an alternative for 'messy play' with limits (such as using pouring toys while the toddler is in the bath or finger painting on a newspaper-covered table) and then sit with the toddler during the resulting tears and tantrums that will ensue, validating the toddler's emotions.

The fear of making our toddlers cry

I understand that it is not nice to know that you, as a parent, have made your toddler cry, but sometimes it is necessary. It is an important part of their development; indeed it is a vital part of their development. Disappointment is an important step for toddlers in learning to live harmoniously in an adult world. Our toddlers need to experience disappointment in order to learn that sometimes they must put the needs of others first. Also, they need to learn that while many rules can be, and should be, challenged, sometimes rules exist for a reason and for these important rules and warnings, particularly those related to our safety, it is important that we follow them.

Why are we so averse to toddlers crying or tantruming? Certainly whenever I am interviewed for an article on toddlers I am always asked, 'How can you avoid toddler tantrums?' I believe that tantrums and tears are not necessarily something to be avoided; rather they are something to be understood and something not to demonise. Toddler tantrums, while deeply annoying to adults, are valid communication methods for toddlers. In our rush to hush them, perhaps we are the ones being disrespectful rather than our toddlers for tantruming in the first place?

Our need, as adults, to keep our toddlers quiet is very often that, **our** need, our embarrassment and our inability to contain our own feelings in order to contain theirs. Certainly, if you were crying and your partner 'shushed' you and said, 'Don't be silly, that's a silly thing to be upset about, you're fine, stop crying,' you would probably recoil and wonder why they were being so rude and disrespectful towards you, so why is it OK to say this to toddlers? When I was growing up my parents used the phrase 'emotionally constipated' about certain people; in our quest to avoid our toddlers expressing their emotions are we encouraging them to grow up to be emotionally constipated? Is our inability to cope with their big emotions, particularly out in public, helpful to our long-term goals for them? What will happen when they are teenagers and in need of a way to release the hurtful feelings inside them? Will they seek out a conversation with us or will they direct that unease inwards, in the form of something like self-harm or an eating disorder, or outwards, in the form of aggressive behaviour? Perhaps then it may be us, the parents, the other adults in society, who need to understand and accept normal toddler behaviour, with public tears and tantrums being at the core of that.

What does parenting with compassion look like?

Those who parent with compassion and respect are not afraid of making their child cry in attempting to reinforce important limits; they are strong enough to cope with the resulting strong emotions that will surface in the toddler. Those who parent with compassion set firm boundaries and are not afraid to reinforce them wherever necessary, nor are they afraid of or angry at their toddler's response when they test these boundaries. Those who parent with compassion know how important it is sometimes to say 'No' or 'Stop'; they don't give their toddlers a cookie just before their dinner because they don't like to upset their child, they don't let their toddler climb over a relative's new sofa because 'they are just exploring and being a toddler'. Those who truly parent with compassion and respect value and understand the need for boundaries and limits as much as they respect and value the need for unconditional love and the importance of exploration for toddlers.

One of our most important goals as a parent is keeping our toddler safe and in order to do this it is important to have boundaries. Toddlers must learn that they cannot run into the road or touch a fire; we need to set limits so that we can protect our children, both in our presence and when they are in the presence of others. We know that toddlers are not yet fully capable of making rational decisions; their immature neocortex does not allow them to weigh up the pros and cons of running out into the road when a car is fast approaching, nor can they accurately judge distance and speed. Our role here is to help them to learn that sometimes the world carries dangers.

Similarly, in order for a toddler to feel safe and comfortable in our presence we need to have an element of authority. Toddlers who are given too much power by their parents can often feel as uncomfortable as those who are given too little; toddlers who are not afforded much control over their own lives can often 'act up' as a way of telling their parents that they need more control, and in much the same way a toddler who needs their parent to take control can also act up.

Toddlers can struggle with making decisions. I'm sure you've experienced the frustration of getting your toddler dressed in the morning only for them to declare 'I don't like these trousers' as soon as they have them on. You allow them to select a different outfit, but as soon as this is on they say 'I don't like this T-shirt any more' before breaking down into tears. This again comes back to their brain development. This struggle with decision-making can be as unsettling to your toddler as it can be frustrating to you, and in order to allay these feelings of unease they need your help in setting them limits. How might you set limits in this scenario?

It could be as simple as giving options: 'Well you can either wear this outfit or this one, which would you prefer?'

In much the same way as toddlers enjoy repetition and the security of a known routine, the same can be said of limits, and having predictable limits in place can help a toddler to feel confident and secure enough to explore the world around him. Of course, it isn't only the setting of limits that is important; maintaining and enforcing them is vital too. Imagine if one day you calmly and gently enforced your limit of not allowing your toddler to empty every single toy out of the toy box by saying, 'I can see you want to play, but remember we take out one toy at a time', and then the next day you were tired and rather than enforcing your limit you allowed the toddler to empty the toy box without saying anything. What message is this giving to your toddler? Especially if you enforce the limit again the very next day. Your toddler will not understand that on the day you didn't enforce the limit it was because you didn't have enough energy; they will just be confused by the fact that one day it was OK for them to empty out all of their toys and another day it wasn't. The fact that they cannot predict your reaction is as unsettling to them as the lack of any other rhythm to their lives.

In ToddlerCalm™ classes we focus on the importance of the rhythm and routine of setting and enforcing limits, including it as part of the 'Rhythm' section of our CRUCIAL framework (see chapter 14).

How to set and enforce effective limits

The real key to setting boundaries and limits is to find a balance, picking those that really matter to you, which keep your toddler safe and help him to learn about the world in which he lives and the behaviour that is expected of him, while also being mindful of his development, needs and feelings. Once you have chosen the limits that are important to you it is vitally important to stick to them every day as a family and also to ensure that anybody who cares for your toddler does the same, and this means discussing and agreeing limits with your partner and any other caregivers, ensuring that they all know what boundaries you have set for your toddler and ensuring that these are enforced, whoever the toddler is with.

This might sound like a daunting task, but it is much easier than it sounds. I think perhaps one of the biggest mistakes parents of toddlers make initially is setting too many limits, being too strict and too quick to pounce on any behaviour that doesn't fit our adult ideals, while we can commonly also become too permissive and not set enough limits through fear of our toddler's response. I would like to reiterate here, don't be afraid to set limits, but select only those that are really important to you first.

A good way of doing this is to write down all of the things that are unacceptable and unsafe for your toddler to do, for instance: running into the road, pulling the dog's tail, hitting their younger sibling, drawing on the walls, bouncing on the sofa, running around the supermarket and refusing to be buckled into their car seat. Then, when you have created your list look at it again and decide if any of the things on your list are less important to you. If they are cross them out for now, and revisit them another day. Decide on the top three limits that are absolutely vital to you, whether that be for safety or other reasons, and begin to implement limit setting with your toddler, making sure that you share this list with your toddler's other caregivers and ensuring that everyone enforces these limits at all times. I'm sure your toddler will protest at first and you will need to sit with them while they cry and tantrum, but in time they will accept these new limits and you will begin to notice that not only do they accept them but also the predictability of them helps your toddler to remain calm. Once you have worked on your top three limits, for example, try adding a new limit each week. Each time make sure that others who care for your toddler are aware of them and enforce them also.

It is important to realise that setting limits is a way of teaching your toddler what is and what isn't acceptable in a sociable world, and this means that you will also need to help them to understand what is acceptable as an alternative. For instance, in the case of pulling the dog's tail, when your toddler does this, first enforce the limit by saying, 'No, we don't pull the dog's tail it hurts him and makes him angry' and then offer instruction on an acceptable alternative: 'He likes it when we stroke him gently like this.' In the case of bouncing on the sofa you could say, 'We don't jump on sofas, they are expensive and it might break them,' and then offer an alternative: 'We can get your mini trampoline out if you want to jump.' In the case of hitting a baby sibling, first enforce the limit by saying, 'Oww, we mustn't hit baby, it hurts and makes him cry' and then offer an alternative: 'If you want to hit you can bang your toy drum.' Don't expect magic results and for your toddler to learn from the first experience because that simply won't happen. Limits need to be constantly enforced; repetition is the key. You might have to remind your toddler that it is unacceptable to pull the dog's tail (and offer an alternative) twenty times before he finally grasps the concept, but if you (and other caregivers) are consistent he **will** grasp it!

THE DIFFERENCE BETWEEN AUTHORITATIVE AND AUTHORITARIAN PARENTING

Many people confuse the terms authoritative and authoritarian, mistakenly thinking that they mean the same thing; however, they do not. Authoritarianism is all about a leader being in control, with those beneath him submitting to his every instruction, whereas authoritative describes somebody with authority who is respected and reliable. Clearly authoritarian parenting is undesirable and is best illustrated by the Victorian style, where children were 'seen but not heard', accepted an adult's instructions without question and called their fathers 'Sir'. Quite often authoritarian parenting is led by fear, or what many call 'fear of God' parenting, with the threat of punishment, sometimes physical, used to control the child and their behaviour. The type of parenting I advocate in this book fits nicely into the authoritative definition, which describes parents who are seen as having a position of authority and afford respect from their child, and they earn this respect from their children by being respectful and empathic towards them. Authoritative parents are not scared to implement boundaries and limits for their children, but they are always enforced with love and respect.

Setting limits is something that parents often ask about in ToddlerCalm™ classes. Very often it is a subject shrouded in mystery for many and they are either too confused or too scared to act in an authoritative manner towards their toddler; sometimes they have already tried setting limits to no avail, but often these limits have failed either because they were not consistently enforced or realistic alternatives offered, often because the parents are busy with an older or younger sibling, work or the everyday demands and stresses of adult life.

Alex's story

My two-and-a-half-year-old son regularly hits me or his older brother. Sometimes he also hits his father or grandma, particularly at times when he is feeling frustrated, but sometimes he hits for no real apparent reason.

I found at first that I reacted very inconsistently at different times, depending on what I was doing and how I was feeling on that particular day. For example, on days when I was feeling fairly calm and patient I would calmly tell him 'No' and sometimes I would choose to completely ignore the punch and try to distract him with a different activity. On other occasions, when I was feeling really tired and wound up, or maybe I was too busy trying to do something important, I would totally lose my cool and shout at him. Some days I felt so angry, when he had hit me for what felt like the hundredth time that day, that I wanted to push him away. None of these reactions, however, made him hit any less.

I felt reluctant to use things like 'time out' or the naughty step, as for some reason they never sat quite right with me and I also didn't feel that I would ever consistently use the techniques, which I presumed would render them pointless. The one time I did put him on the stairs his brother immediately turned to me and said, 'Should I go and give him a cuddle?' My older son's response then of course confirmed to me that this sort of punishment was a completely unnatural 'solution' and one that wouldn't work for us. The other problem was that sometimes, when he hit his brother, his brother would naturally scream and shout, but at other times he would say, 'It's OK, I don't mind, it doesn't really hurt.' This made me even madder and I felt like screaming, 'It is **not** OK!'

I have recently decided to make a massive effort with responding exactly the same way every time he hits. I have started to tell him: 'No hitting, it hurts, it makes people feel sad when you hit.' The idea that what he is doing makes me or his brother feel sad really seems to get him thinking. He often replies, 'No, Mummy, you're not sad . . . ?' I then tell him, 'If you're angry and you need to hit something, hit the bean bag.' He tends to then go and jump on the bean bag, which I think helps him to vent some energy and aggression. I have also explained to his brother that this is what we are going to do now and that we need always to respond in the same way. It is still really hard; sometimes I feel like my blood is boiling. I do try to remind myself though that my getting really angry doesn't work and actually makes him more aggressive. I'm starting to see a difference and knowing that I'm being consistent is helping me to stay calm and more in focus, which is calming him too I think. I have also recently started an evening class once a week. This gives me a much appreciated break from being 'on duty' at home. I think it is having a really positive effect on my patience and energy levels for coping with the challenges of my toddler.

Chapter 14

CRUCIAL in action: ten worked examples for common toddler concerns

The law of love could be best understood and learned through little children.

Mohatma Ghandi

The aim of this chapter is not to show you 'the answer' for common toddler problems, because there is no 'one size fits all', and the best way to handle your concerns about your own toddler will be to realise that they are unique to you and your family and to consider the individuality of your toddler and their environment. The aim here is to show you how each of the points in the CRUCIAL framework can be used to apply to many different issues faced by the parents of toddlers. I will take you through ten examples. The basic advice is the same, so read Example 1 carefully for the framework and read through the other examples for more specific details.

The suggestions given here are not the only solutions; I am sure there are ideas I haven't thought of and you have probably already tried some of the suggestions and decided that they do not work for your family. Use them as a starting point to work through the framework to find solutions that are unique to your family. I hope I have covered most of the major concerns parents of toddlers have, but if your particular worry is not mentioned here you can work through my CRUCIAL framework yourself and apply each letter to your concern. Just to remind you at the outset, the CRUCIAL words are Control, Rhythm, Understanding, Communication, Individual, Avoidance and Love.

Example 1: The biting and/ or hitting toddler

This is a top concern of many parents. It is bad enough if your toddler is hit or bitten by another, but it is so much more distressing if your own toddler is the hitter or the biter. Perhaps your toddler might hit or bite other toddlers at playgroup, perhaps the hitting or biting is directed at you, or perhaps it is directed at an older or younger sibling. Your toddler may hit or bite rarely, or it may be a daily occurrence. Working through the CRUCIAL framework can give you a good idea of not only the reasons why your toddler may hit or bite, but what you can do to solve the problem.

Control

Biting and hitting can be common symptoms of a child who is desperate to have more **control** over their life or a certain situation. Very often the behaviour is as a result of frustration, so enabling your toddler to have a little more control over their days can often have tremendously positive effects. Has the biting or hitting behaviour started after the arrival of a new sibling, your return to work or the starting of preschool, for example? In all of these instances the toddler may feel out of control and also feel a need to reconnect more to their parents.

To re-establish that connection and to help your toddler feel in control, spend ten minutes of one-to-one playtime together each day, preferably with just you and your toddler. Remember that the aim of this playtime is that your toddler will be in complete control, choosing whether you play with him and choosing what you play. Your goal here is to encourage these feelings of control in your toddlers and to engage in whatever play he asks of you. Let your toddler know he has your undivided attention for the ten minutes of 'special playtime' and when it comes to an end remind him that you will play again tomorrow.

Rhythm

Rhythm is all about predictability. Creating rhythm and patterns of the day and week give your toddler a sense of control over their day, and by knowing what comes next your toddler feels safer and more comfortable, which in turn is less likely to result in anxious behaviour such as biting and hitting. If the hitting and biting occurs after the arrival of a new baby sibling try to stick to your toddler's daily routine as much as possible, rather than fitting your lives around the new arrival. Sometimes toddlers can hit and bite during holidays, either holidays away or those spent at home away from preschool and nursery. This may be as a result of their routine being disrupted, which in turn leads your toddler to lose that reassuring predictability, leaving him feeling unstable. Trying to stick to a similar routine at home can really help.

Also remember that setting limits and enforcing them is a vital part of giving your toddler a predictable rhythm to their life. In the case of hitting and/or biting make sure that you have an appropriate limit in place that is enforced, in the same way, by all of those people who are close to your toddler. As soon as your toddler begins to hit or bite loudly say, 'Oww, we don't bite it hurts, it makes Mummy cry' or 'Stop, we never hit the baby, it could really hurt her.' These limits then need to be immediately followed up with a more acceptable alternative, for instance, 'You can hit your special angry cushion if you need to hit something' or 'Remember your biting ring, if you want to bite please use that.' You could also offer them a choice of alternative objects that they can bite, for instance a teething ring, a teething necklace or another safe toy that can withstand biting. In the case of hitting you could offer the choice of a special cushion, a toy drum or a big squashy ball to hit. Letting your toddler choose their own 'angry object' can help them feel more in control and once the object is in place they have the security of knowing which object to use when they feel angry and need to hit or bite.

Understanding

When you **understand** why your child is biting or hitting you will be well on the way towards solving the problem. There are many possible reasons, almost an infinite number, which is frustrating. Perhaps he is teething and biting helps to relieve the pressure behind his gums; perhaps he is undergoing a sensory period of development and the biting or hitting literally feels good and interesting; or perhaps the biting or hitting behaviour is indicating an unmet need, maybe for more attention from you, or maybe for more exercise and entertainment. Always remember though that your toddler is not biting or hitting to be deliberately malicious or to annoy you; he is not 'a spiteful child'.

Communication

As with understanding, biting and hitting behaviour can be a sign that your child is trying to **communicate** something to you, particularly if his language capabilities are not strong and he is having trouble making his needs known to you. In this case you could perhaps consider using some basic sign language or a set of cards or toys depicting different emotions, so that your toddler can show you which one he is feeling.

Think about how you communicate with your toddler. Remember the 'say what you see' approach: 'I see a little boy who is very angry that his toy was stolen from him.' Communicate that biting/hitting hurts (a very loud 'OWW, THAT HURT' immediately afterwards), followed by naming their emotions: 'I know you are angry that little Johnny stole your toy but biting hurts' and then offering an alternative, 'We don't bite people, but you can bite your teething necklace if you want to bite.' Always keep communication consistent too; remember it takes time to change behaviour in this way. Remember to make sure that both parents and other caregivers take the same approach.

Think about the theory of modelling when considering your response. If you are violent to your child, whether that be through the commonly advocated 'biting back' or 'giving a good smack because he needs to learn what it feels like', all you are really teaching your child is to copy you and showing them that biting or hitting is acceptable. If it is not acceptable for our toddlers to bite or hit others why do so many people believe it is acceptable to bite or hit them in order to 'teach them a lesson'? This is something I will never understand.

Individual

As with understanding, where there are so many reasons why toddlers bite and hit, it is impossible to give one answer as your toddler is an **individual**; therefore it is important you consider their situation when deciding what to do. Your toddler may not bite for the same reason that a friend's toddler bites. Your toddler may not hit for the same reason that your older child hit. With this in mind your response has to be individual and tailored to your toddler and their unique situation. What worked for a friend or an older child may not work for your toddler.

Avoidance

If your toddler persistently bites or hits at playgroup, perhaps **avoiding** the playgroup for a while could be a good idea. If you remove the stimulus you can often naturally remove the response; this may only be temporary and taking a short break may give your toddler enough time to outgrow the behaviour and give you enough of a break that you feel better able to cope with it.

If your toddler is becoming visibly distressed on a playdate and you feel that his behaviour will soon deteriorate into biting or hitting don't feel that you need to see out the rest of the play-date, and cut it short. Ultimately it is about showing your toddler respect for his needs and having the courage to take the appropriate action in order to stop him resorting to less appropriate behaviour to communicate these needs to you.

Love

Always remember that it is your toddler's biting or hitting that you dislike, not your toddler. Your toddler is not doing it to deliberately annoy you. If you can help your toddler to feel unconditionally **loved** and accepted he will feel less need to resort to more destructive behaviour to seek your attention.

In the case of biting and hitting, it is also really important to think about self-love. In order to cope with your toddler's challenging behaviour and big feelings it is important for you to empty your own container. Biting and hitting is incredibly stressful and many parents are overly hard on themselves, wondering what they did to breed such an antisocial toddler. If you combine this with the anxiety, stress and embarrassment of dealing with this behaviour, it is very easy to end up feeling emotionally wrung out and exhausted, and far less capable of providing your toddler with the support that he really needs. Make sure you get support too and find a way to nurture yourself and take a break from your toddler if you need to.

Try to not to pay too much attention to what others may say about your toddler, and don't let their opinions or advice worry you or change how you feel about your toddler.

Example 2: The toddler who throws everything

Many parents are concerned that their toddler throws everything that they can lay their hands on, often throwing objects at other people, and breaking lots of things in the process too. Obviously it is not acceptable to hurt others, nor is it acceptable to break your favourite possessions. So what can you do to stem the throwing? Working through the CRUCIAL framework can help you here too.

Control

Toddlers who persistently throw inappropriate objects at inappropriate times can be frustrated, therefore if you enable your toddler to have a little more **control** over their days you often notice that the throwing behaviour dramatically reduces. Establish the one-to-one playtime sessions as mentioned in Example 1.

You can also help your toddler to have a little more control by giving them choices. After telling them that it is not acceptable to throw whatever item is their current weapon, you could then offer them a choice of alternative objects that they can throw, for instance a soft ball or a beanbag. You could also give them the option to go outside if they want to be more vigorous with their throwing or want to throw something a little harder, for instance a football.

Rhythm

Creating **rhythm** in a toddler's life is all about predictability, which is likely to reduce anxious behaviour such as throwing. Refer back to Example 1 for advice.

In the case of inappropriate throwing set a limit in place that is enforced, in the same way, by all of those people who are close to your toddler. As soon as your toddler begins to try to throw something inappropriate in a place that is not appropriate to throw, calmly tell them, 'Stop, we don't throw inside' or 'Stop, we don't throw shoes, they hurt people' or 'Stop, we never throw things at the baby, it could really hurt her.' These limits then need to be immediately followed up with a more acceptable alternative, for instance, 'You can throw your beanbag inside' or 'If you want to throw we can go into the garden and play with your football.'

Understanding

Try to **understand** why your child is throwing everything, or why they want to throw objects indoors so much; there are so many potential reasons here, but if you can uncover the cause you are so much closer to solving the problem. Perhaps your toddler is developing a new schema (an understanding of the world) and is being a typical 'little scientist' by learning about the world through his actions. Think about how much throwing teaches us, such as gravity, distance, weight and so on.

Throwing is commonly linked to your toddler needing to get outside and burn off energy more than they perhaps do already. Think of your toddler as being like a puppy trapped inside all day; they will quickly get bored and resort to destructive behaviour. Always remember though that your toddler is not throwing things to be deliberately malicious, there is always a reason behind their behaviour.

Communication

Your toddler's throwing can be a sign that he is trying to **communicate** something to you. If his language capabilities are not strong he may well be having trouble communicating these needs to you, here you could consider using basic sign language, gestures, books or physical clues to help your toddler to feel heard. Similarly how you communicate with your toddler is vital, remember the 'say what you see' approach we discussed earlier. 'I know you enjoy throwing but we can't throw heavy things inside' and then offering an alternative: 'You can throw this beanbag inside, or we can go outside and throw your football.' Always keep communication consistent too; it takes time to change behaviour in this way. It is also particularly important that both parents take the same approach.

Individual

As ever, it is impossible to give one answer to solve the problem of toddlers who throw, as your toddler is an **individual**; therefore it is important you consider their unique situation when deciding what to do. Your toddler may not throw for the same reason as your friend's toddler, so it may not be appropriate for you to handle the behaviour in the same way as your friend.

Avoidance

If your toddler throws things at other people's houses on playdates, **avoiding** playdates altogether for a while could be a good idea. It could give you both the break you need in order diffuse the situation, as a result you may feel calmer and confident, and this will have a knock-on effect on your toddler.

Also, try to see if your toddler's behaviour occurs at a particular time of day, for instance does he only throw when his sibling is around? This could be him trying to signal that he needs more one-to-one time with you, or perhaps he throws when he is hungry or tired, in which case you could try to avoid the behaviour by trying to spot the signs before his behaviour deteriorates.

Love

As always remember it is the throwing you dislike, not your toddler. Keep reminding yourself that, although it certainly may feel like it at times, he is not doing it to deliberately annoy you. Remember always to try to **love** your toddler unconditionally in order to help him feel secure and validated, and then the unwanted behaviour is less likely to occur.

Parenting a toddler who constantly throws can be very stressful so try to make sure that you get support too and find a way to nurture yourself and take a break from your toddler if you need to. Refer to the advice I gave in Example 1 for ways to ensure you give enough love to yourself.

Example 3: The toddler who doesn't share anything

I think every parent of a toddler has experienced this at some point. I vividly remember the embarrassment I felt at playgroup when my toddler was overly possessive with the toys he was playing with; any attempt from me to make him share was inevitably followed by tears or tantrums. I lost count of the number of times that I apologised for him.

Control

Think about how little **control** your toddler has over his life and how unsettling it must be for him to be at playgroup enthralled with a toy that he has found, only to have another child take it from him or, perhaps even worse, for you to tell him that he must now share it. He is almost powerless here to stop the plaything that he has been so enjoying being taken from him. This is even worse if the toy belongs to him.

You can help your child to have a little more control here by giving him choices, for instance you could ask him to pick another toy to share with the other child instead, or perhaps you could use an egg timer, which he can control, telling him 'when the sand runs out you need to let little Johnny play with the toy'. If you have friends coming to your house for a playdate give your toddler the option of packing away toys that are special to him that he doesn't want other children to play with in advance of the other child's arrival. Giving him the control to choose the toys that will remain out can have very positive effects.

Rhythm

Remember that setting limits and enforcing them is a vital part of giving your toddler a predictable rhythm to their life. In the case of a toddler who is possessive over objects make sure that you have an appropriate limit in place that is enforced, in the same way, by all of those people who are close to your toddler. If your toddler is having trouble taking turns with another child you could say, 'Johnny really wants to play with the toy now, he's very sad that he can't play' and then immediately follow this with an alternative, for instance, 'Can you find another toy for Johnny to play with?' or 'Shall we use the egg timer to help us to decide when to give the toy to Johnny?'

Understanding

It is very important to try to **understand** why your child doesn't want to share. Perhaps they are just so fascinated with the toy that they don't want to give it up. Remember, also, that toddlers are incredibly egocentric. As we saw in chapter 2, toddlers can only see the world through their eyes, so they do not understand that by not sharing they are making little Johnny sad; they just don't think like adults do.

Sharing is actually quite a mature concept and skill to grasp and one that comes much later in life, usually once your child starts school. Understanding here that it is totally normal for toddlers not to share is very helpful. Once you understand this you also understand why it is completely pointless forcing your toddler to apologise to the other child. Your toddler will have no grasp of the other child's feelings or consequences of their refusal to share and because of this they are not truly sorry, even if they repeat the words, parrot fashion, that you have told them to say. Indeed, forcing toddlers to say sorry is entirely for the benefit of adults, as it does nothing to benefit your toddler, or the other toddler.

Communication

Remember how you **communicate** with your toddler is vital; here is a good time to use the 'say what you see' approach and also to think again about the theory of modelling. If you model kind and sharing behaviour yourself and name your toddler's emotions: 'I can see you love that toy and know that you are really sad that little Johnny wants to play with it too,' your toddler is more likely to grasp the concept of empathy, and thus sharing, sooner. If you empathise with your toddler and show them that you understand how they are feeling you help to validate their emotions and help them to feel secure and that it's OK for them to feel these strong emotions.

Also think carefully about the words you use related to sharing. Sometimes we may tell our toddlers to 'share your chocolate' or 'share your sandwich', but when they share something edible it is obvious that they will not get back the part of the food that they shared. When we ask a toddler to 'share your toy', we may unwittingly be indicating to them that they will not get the toy back. Perhaps better words to use here would be 'give some of your chocolate' and 'give some of your sandwich' and then 'take turns to play with your toy'. Your toddler will then feel safer in the knowledge that they will get their toy back.

Individual

As always, remember your toddler is an **individual**, and it is important you consider their situation when deciding what to do. Consider the stage of development they are at, and whether a particular social behaviour is really something that you should expect from your child. Certainly you should not compare the sharing capabilities of a three-year-old with a four-year-old and, even between children of the same age, no two children reach exactly the same stage of development at exactly the same time. Your toddler is unique and will grasp the concept of empathy and sharing in his own time.

Avoidance

If your toddler gets stressed over sharing toys on playdates, **avoiding** them for a while could be a good idea. Also, try to avoid any situations with your child's own toys, particularly their favourite ones, by not taking them out in public or putting them away when a friend comes over for a playdate.

Love

As always remember it is the behaviour you dislike, not your toddler. Look back to the advice given in Example 1 for the **Love** aspect of the CRUCIAL framework.

Example 4: The toddler who won't get dressed or let you change their nappy

Lots of toddlers can be uncooperative when it comes to getting dressed or allowing you to change their nappy. The stress that parents experience with an uncooperative toddler is only exacerbated if they have another child to care for or are in a rush to leave the house. So what can you do to encourage your toddler to get dressed or allow you to change their nappy? Working through the CRUCIAL framework can give you a good idea of not only the reasons why your toddler may be uncooperative with this, but what you can do to resolve the issue.

Control

This is perhaps the most important point for both of these scenarios. You can help your child to have a little **control**, which often results in much more cooperation, by giving them choices. You could let them choose their own clothes within reason, but really, is it so bad if they go to playgroup in a fairy outfit or to the beach in wellington boots? And let them dress themselves wherever possible.

In the case of changing a nappy, try offering your toddler a choice of 'We need to change your nappy, shall we do it before your favourite show comes on or during the adverts?' They could also choose where the nappy change takes place, or perhaps even choose their own change mat. You could also give them little jobs, for instance, putting their nappy into the bin or nappy bucket after the change; this all helps them to feel more in control.

Both of these behaviours may indicate that your toddler has

a need to be more in control in other aspects of their life too, so have a think about any other ways you could help your toddler to feel more in control, such as joining in 'special time' and free play with your toddler each day.

Rhythm

Nappy changing is a great time to introduce a ritual and **rhythm** into your toddler's routine. You could make up a 'nappy changing song' and sing it together while the changing is happening: 'This is the way we wipe the poo, wipe the poo, wipe the poo' (sung to the tune of 'Here we go round the Mulberry Bush') is a good one to try.

You could make getting dressed into a fun game, by giving your toddler the task of naming parts of the body while they are getting dressed. For instance: You: 'Where do your knickers/pants go?' Toddler: 'My pants/knickers go on my bottom'; You: 'Where is your bottom?' Toddler: 'Here!'; You: 'Can you put your pants on your bottom?' The more you can make getting dressed into a game and the more fun you make it the more likely it is that your toddler will want to get involved.

In the case of refusing to lie still or reaching into their nappy during nappy changes, or refusing to get dressed, make sure you have an appropriate limit in place that will be enforced, in the same way, by all of those people who are close to your toddler. During nappy changes, as soon as your toddler begins to squirm, or his hands head towards the poo, say, 'I need you to stay still during nappy changes because I don't like getting poo on my hands.' These limits then need to be immediately followed up with a more acceptable alternative, for instance, 'If you are bored you can play with your toy while I finish.' You can also help your toddler to have a little more control by offering him a choice of alternative objects he can play with during nappy changing, I know some parents even have special 'nappy changing toys' that only come out at nappy change time.

Understanding

Try to **understand** how your child is feeling, for instance having a nappy changed must feel pretty yucky and cold, perhaps the wipes or cream that you use sting, or perhaps they did in the past. And your toddler is therefore possibly frightened of nappy change time for fear they will be in pain. Or perhaps they hate having to lie still on the floor when they would rather be playing or running around.

For toddlers, having to get dressed is often a boring chore that takes them away from something more fun and many just love to be naked. Perhaps they don't like the feel of waistbands on their tummy, scratchy labels in their tops or just how clothing inhibits their movement. I know I stopped putting dresses and skirts on my daughter when she was very young as they used to really inhibit her crawling and climbing; she was much happier therefore in trousers that allowed her to move freely.

Communication

The 'say what you see' **communication** approach works well here, for instance 'I see that you are busy playing, but your bottom is very smelly and if we don't change your nappy it might make you sore' or 'Darling I can see you are enjoying this programme, but I need you to get dressed now as we are going out.'

Also think about effective praise here. 'I'm so proud that you let me change your nappy, I know you were busy playing and it was hard for you to leave your game and lay still on the floor' or

'Wow, I know you really didn't want to get dressed then because your favourite programme was on. I am so thankful that you allowed me to dress you, it has made the morning so much easier.'

Consider using self-modelling too. When you get dressed in the morning you could say, 'I'm really proud of myself for getting dressed each day, even though I find it quite boring doing it.' Yes, you will feel slightly crazy saying it, but your toddler will hear you and we all know how much they like to copy us.

Individual

As always it is important you consider your toddler's **individual** situation when deciding what to do about the problem. Maybe your toddler doesn't like nappy changes because the wipes are cold or lying on the floor is uncomfortable? Maybe he or she doesn't like the scratchy label in the back of their vest? Try never to compare your toddler with other toddlers.

Avoidance

You can't **avoid** getting dressed or changing a nappy, but you can pick your battles, for instance does it really matter if your toddler goes out in red trousers, green shoes, a pink top and a blue hat? We might be embarrassed at their lack of colour co-ordination, but if you avoid having a stressful morning does it really matter?

Ask yourself, 'Why am I insisting that my toddler do this?' If the answer is 'to keep him safe, to keep others safe, to keep him healthy, or to help him to learn about the world he lives in' then it is important that you enforce limits on the behaviour, but if your answer is something more akin to 'because I am embarrassed or people will stare if I take him out like this' then perhaps you may want to reconsider how important it is for your toddler to do as you ask in this case.

Love

It is the behaviour/refusal to get dressed/lie still that you dislike, not your toddler. Look back to the advice given in Example 1 for the **Love** aspect of the CRUCIAL framework.

Example 5: The toddler who won't eat anything

Many parents despair over their toddler's picky eating. They spend hours preparing food to tempt their toddler to eat, and worry that their toddler is not eating enough vitamins and minerals to stay healthy or consuming enough calories in order to grow and be strong. Concerns over your toddler's eating habits can very quickly consume your life. What can you do to encourage your toddler to eat more and make healthy choices? Working through the CRUCIAL framework can give you a good idea of not only the reasons why your toddler may refuse to eat, but what you can do to cope with the issue.

Control

The element of **control** is vitally important here. It is very likely that your toddler has very little control over their food intake, even though you may think that their eating behaviour is highly controlling. As parents, we often decide what our toddlers eat, including choosing the temperature the food is served at and what plate it is served on, and we control the quantity of each item and the overall portion size. We tend to control when they eat and where they eat, as well as even controlling how they eat it, often telling them, 'Please use your cutlery and not your fingers.' Sometimes we even spoon the food into our toddler's mouths, effectively giving them no control at all, which can actually be pretty scary for them.

Giving a child control over their food intake can make a massive difference to their eating habits and the problems that we experience with them. In reality this may involve letting them pick the food they want to eat, within reason and some flexible limits, allowing them to choose the quantities of the food that they eat, whether they eat it hot or cold, when they eat, as opposed to only offering food at set mealtimes, allowing them to tell us when they are no longer hungry and allowing them to help us to prepare their food.

One of the best ways to cope with toddler eating habits is to make up a 'grazing box'. At the start of your day you simply fill the box with prepared nutritious food that you are happy for your toddler to eat and leave it in a place that they can access freely throughout the day (a low shelf in the fridge for instance). This affords them a huge amount of control over their eating behaviour and allows them to eat intuitively when they are hungry, selecting what they eat and how much. You will often find that your toddler will graze from their box throughout the day, taking small amounts at a time, but at the end of the day you will most likely discover that they have actually eaten quite a lot, and usually quite healthily, in total.

Rhythm

We know that **rhythm** is all about predictability, and knowing what comes next helps your toddler feel safer and more comfortable, so this is a great time to introduce a family ritual, to prepare for eating, which could start with setting the table and hand washing. Again you could perhaps make up a song indicating that food is arriving soon.

Setting limits and enforcing them is vital here. In the case of your toddler refusing to eat any savoury food and demanding nothing but sweetened yogurt, make sure that you have an appropriate limit in place that is enforced, in the same way, by all of those people who are close to your toddler. When your toddler demands yoghurt you could say, 'I know you love yoghurt, darling, but you do need to eat something else too.' These limits then need to be immediately followed up with a more acceptable alternative, for instance, 'What would you like to have to go with your yoghurt? I can make you some pasta or a sandwich.'

Understanding

Trying to **understand** why your child will not eat is no mean feat. Maybe they aren't hungry, maybe they don't like the food you are offering, maybe they only like cold food, maybe they like to eat little and often: very often the reasons change daily for toddlers. Whatever the reason though, respecting your child's natural appetite is really important, but can be very hard to do, because as adults we have become accustomed to eat to the clock, to eat socially and to eat because we think we should. Trusting our toddler's natural eating habits is a difficult skill for us to master, but once you have it makes everything so much easier.

Communication

Using the 'say what you see' approach shows your toddler you have noticed what they are doing but importantly when it comes to eating you are not praising them for it. We have seen that it is important that you try not to create a child who only eats to please you. So rather than, 'Good girl, you ate up your lunch,' instead you could say, 'I can see that you are enjoying that sandwich and that you have eaten quite a lot of cucumber.'

Remember too that your body language is **communication**; if mealtimes are stressful for you your toddler is very likely to pick up on your tension, so try to diffuse the emotions that surround food for both yourself and your toddler. Ideally eating should be emotion-free; if we view food as fuel and eating as your toddler asserting their natural instincts then it becomes just that, rather than a daily battle to be won.

Individual

Remember that food is a very **individual** thing; appetites vary even day to day, some days your toddler might be really hungry, sometimes they may have no appetite at all, taste buds change too and some toddlers can even be more sensitive to bitter tastes than others. Your toddler's eating behaviour will not be the same as yours, your partner's, your other children's, your friends' children's or the supposedly 'normal' toddler written about in other books. There is no 'normal' when it comes to toddler eating; it is all about individual preferences. The hardest part of parenting a picky eater is accepting them for who they are rather than trying to change them to fit our expectations.

Avoidance

If food is a big issue for you and your toddler try to **avoid** placing any more stress on it. For instance don't try to feed your toddler in a rush; it will only make both of you more stressed and lead him to eat even less. Graze boxes work well 'on the run' and I have taken them into the car with me many times, which has avoided the trauma of trying to get a toddler to eat quickly so that you can attend an important appointment.

Love

As always, remember it is the behaviour you dislike, not your toddler. They are not being 'picky' deliberately to annoy you. Look back to the advice given in Example 1 for the **Love** aspect of the CRUCIAL framework.

Example 6: The toddler who won't sleep through the night

Many parents struggle with the issue of night waking throughout the toddler years and, for some, while night waking may not be a problem, they have trouble putting their toddler to bed at night, some struggle to keep their toddler in their room, and very quickly these behaviours can leave the whole family distressed and exhausted. Using the CRUCIAL framework can help you to see light at the end of the sleep deprivation tunnel.

Control

As with many other tricky toddler behaviours, sleep issues can often be linked to the toddler having a lack of **control** over their life. With this in mind, if you help your child by allowing them to control some elements of bedtime it may make things a little easier, for instance this could be letting your toddler choose their pyjamas, choose a favourite toy to sleep with, or choose whether to leave the light on or off and, perhaps, if it is something you feel comfortable with, allowing them to choose where they sleep, which for many toddlers is likely to be in your room and sometimes in your bed.

Quite commonly sleep issues can occur after the arrival of a new sibling, a mother's return to work or the starting of pre-school. Establish the one-to-one playtime sessions as mentioned in Example 1.

Rhythm

Rhythm is hugely important in relation to sleep issues. As we have already discussed in chapter 3 of this book, a predictable wind-down routine and a bedtime ritual is very comforting to a child, particularly when the elements are conditioned and are there constantly. Knowing what comes next helps your toddler feel safer and more comfortable, so this is a great time to introduce a ritual, such as my ToddlerCalm™ three step bedtime ritual described in chapter 3. Also, you could perhaps make up a song indicating that bedtime is arriving soon.

Remember, too, that setting limits and enforcing them is a vital part of giving your toddler a predictable rhythm to their life. In the case of your toddler refusing to go to bed, make sure that you have an appropriate limit in place that is enforced, in the same way, by all of those people who are close to your toddler. When your toddler tantrums as bedtime approaches you could say, 'I know you are having fun and would love to stay up, but sleep is very important to keep us healthy.' These limits then need to be immediately followed up with a more acceptable alternative, for instance, 'Would you like to brush your teeth and change into your pyjamas now and then have five more minutes with your toy before bedtime or would you like to play with your toy now for five minutes and then brush your teeth and change into your pyjamas?'

Understanding

I think this is possibly the most important point to grasp when it comes to toddler sleep concerns. If we, as parents, can **understand** that most of us, through no fault of our own, have completely unrealistic expectations of a toddler's sleep we can ease so much worry and stress for the whole family.

We have already seen how science tells us that around half of all toddlers still wake regularly throughout the night at two years of age and in fact it is not really until the age of four that a child's sleep becomes as reliable as and similar to that of an adult. Also, trying to view the world through your toddler's eyes helps you to understand also that the toddler might be scared alone; perhaps there may be a shadow on their wall that frightens them or perhaps they actually may be ready to start the day at 5am, even though we as parents are exhausted and need them to sleep later.

If you revise your understanding and expectations of your toddler's sleeping behaviour perhaps this may help you to make a change in your own behaviour in order to help you to cope, rather than trying to change your toddler's normal sleep patterns and needs. I believe this is the key to surviving the sleepless nights of toddlerdom.

Communication

Sleep problems, or what we perceive as sleep problems, can actually be a sign that your child is trying to **communicate** something to you. They may be feeling insecure, they may be feeling scared, they may be telling you that they need to be closer to you.

If you can understand what your toddler is trying to communicate to you the solutions can be much more obvious.

When it comes to communication I get a little confused regarding night-time parenting. Why is it OK for our toddler to communicate their needs to us in the daytime, but at night we expect them to 'self-soothe' and not need us? Surely night-time, with its accompanying darkness, funny shadows and creaky noises, is a time when toddlers need to communicate with us the most? Since when did parenting only happen between 7am and 7pm? If we consistently return a child to their bedroom at night with limited eye or body contact and limited speech, what are we really communicating to them? If we ignore their cries, what are we communicating to them? What would you hope to communicate to your child? I would imagine you would wish to say that you love them and are always there for them. We would surely hope always to communicate this to our toddlers? Not just for 50 per cent of each day?

Individual

There are so many reasons why toddlers find it hard to get to sleep, wake in the night and rise early. There is a very large natural developmental aspect, but still I would suggest forgetting what your friends' toddlers do and focus only on your **individual** toddler. Also, remember that sleep is only a problem if it is a problem for you and your family, not just because the last book you read said so, or somebody told you so!

Avoidance

If your toddler doesn't sleep well in their own bedroom, but sleeps really well in your room, you might consider **avoiding** the problem and rooming in with them for a bit. Perhaps putting their mattress on your floor or inviting them into your bed, or if you have older children consider 'rooming in' siblings. Similarly, if your toddler sleeps well with a pacifier, but now you've decided it's time they give the dummy up, consider avoiding the 'problem' for a while, until they are ready to sleep without a dummy perhaps. The same can be said of night-time toilet training.

If your toddler is scared of shadows on the wall of their room, it might be possible to avoid this by leaving a light on in their room and if they don't like how quiet it is at night this could be avoided by playing soft music in their room overnight.

Love

As always, remember it is the sleep behaviour you dislike, not your toddler. Look back to the advice given in Example 1 for the **Love** aspect of the CRUCIAL framework.

Example 7: The toddler who tantrums constantly

We've all been there: for reasons you often struggle to understand your toddler bursts into tears and throws themselves dramatically onto the floor wailing, right in the middle of the shop with many onlookers tutting at both you and your ill-behaved child. There's no getting away from it, tantrums are distressing for both parents and toddlers, but what can you do? Using the CRUCIAL framework will help you to understand why your toddler tantrums and how you can ultimately help him to express his feelings in more productive ways.

Control

As with many other tricky toddler behaviours, tantrums can often be linked to the toddler having a lack of **control** over their life. With this in mind, if you help your child to have control by allowing them to control more of their life, it may make things a little easier. Establish the one-to-one playtime sessions as mentioned in Example 1.

Try to also give your toddler as many choices as you can, for instance if tantrums always ensue when you are shopping you could offer your toddler the following choice, 'Would you like to sit in the trolley, carry a basket or walk and hold the trolley?' Similarly you could give your toddler a 'special job' to do in the supermarket, picking the items off the shelves, using the hand held scanner or packing (non-breakable) items. Giving your toddler this element of responsibility can help him to feel important and give him a sense of much needed control. You could also let your toddler have some control over when you actually go shopping, for instance: 'I can see you are busy playing now, we need to go to the shops to get some dinner, would you like to go now or in ten minutes when you have finished your jigsaw?'

Rhythm

It must be so strange for a toddler, not knowing what comes next in their life. **Rhythm** in the toddler's life gives them more control, which in turn can help them to feel safer and more comfortable and less likely to need to use tantrums as a way of asserting more control over their life.

Helping your toddler to understand that 'Tuesday is shopping day', for example, can be really helpful. You could do this by using a pictorial calendar showing 'What we are doing today', or by discussing and planning the shopping trip at bed-time the night before, and reminding them that in the morning 'We are going to the shops'. Rhythms are also about being flex-ible though, so if when your toddler wakes they seem under the weather or overly tired consider postponing your trip, as inevitably a trip with a grumpy, poorly toddler is not going to end well.

Also remember that setting limits and enforcing them is a vital part of giving your toddler a predictable rhythm to their life. In the case of your toddler having constant tantrums, make sure that you have an appropriate limit in place that is enforced in the same way by everyone close to your toddler. When your toddler tantrums in the supermarket because you won't allow them to eat an item you have just picked from the shelves but not yet paid for you could say, 'I know you are hungry and this bread looks yummy, but I haven't paid for it yet so I can't let you have it yet.' These limits then need to be immediately followed up with a more acceptable alternative, for instance, 'I do have a banana in my bag, would you like to eat that now and you can have some bread as soon as we've paid for it?'

Understanding

Understanding what normal toddler behaviour is, and tantrum-ing is just that – normal toddler behaviour – can go a long way to helping you to cope with it. If you understand how your tod-dler's brain develops and what he is physically capable of doing and understanding, your expectations are naturally lowered, and with a new sense of empathy it is much easier to relate to your toddler's behaviour and needs. We know that toddlers do not have the ability to regulate their own emotions and behaviour in the same way as adults, because the part of their brain that regulates behaviour is not fully formed. This means that they literally 'flip out' during a tantrum and even if they wanted to control their feelings and calm down, they can't. Tantrums are very normal and a side effect of immature toddler brain development and I can almost guarantee that they are as scary and stressful to your toddler as they are to you, I'm sure your toddler would rather they didn't tantrum either. When you think of it like that tantrums become much easier to cope with, for both of you.

Communication

A tantrum is a sign that your toddler is trying to **communicate** something to you, usually big, overwhelming feelings, whether that be 'I'm tired', 'I'm bored', 'This place is scary, I don't like all the people', 'I don't want to sit in the trolley, and I'm hungry' or something else. Whether we like it or not, tantrums are a valid form of communication for toddlers. With their limited neural functioning and their limited language capabilities they need to resort to other methods to communicate. If a tantrum is valid communication then surely it would make sense that we do not ignore a toddler who tantrums, or, even worse, punish him for trying to communicate his dis-ease to us?

Try to help your child to communicate to you wherever possible. Use the 'say what you see' approach, to help your toddler to understand and name emotions, for instance, 'I can see you don't like it here, let's try to get what we need and get you out of here as quickly as we can.' Try to describe the behaviour you want from your toddler, 'We use gentle, soft voices,' rather than telling them what you don't want, 'Stop whining.' If you communicate to your toddler with respect and empathy you will be modelling to them the behaviour you expect to see from them in return. Be the behaviour you want to see in your toddler and they are far more likely to mirror you.

Individual

As with understanding there are so many reasons why toddlers tantrum, it is impossible to give one answer as your toddler is an **individual**, so it is important you consider their unique situation when deciding what to do. Along with this, remember that your toddler's physical and psychological development is also unique. Just because no other toddler in the shop is having a tantrum it doesn't mean that there is something wrong with your toddler, it just means that they are all different, they all experience the world in different ways and they all have their own triggers for boredom, fear, discomfort, anger and sadness, just as adults do.

Avoidance

I often ask parents, 'Do you really need to go to the shops today? Could you order online? Could you go tonight when your toddler is in bed? Could you get a takeaway?' when they ask me what they can do to stop their toddler having a tantrum when out. **Avoiding** the trigger seems like such an obvious solution. If you know the supermarket always elicits tantrums in your toddler is it possible to avoid it? Perhaps the behaviour is worse when your toddler is tired or hungry? In that case try to plan your day to go after their nap or lunchtime. Avoidance is much related to the Rhythm section; learn your toddler's individual rhythms and try to work your day around them as much as possible, avoiding trigger times.

Love

As always remember it is the tantrum that you dislike, not your toddler. Look back to the advice given in Example 1 for the **Love** aspect of the CRUCIAL framework.

Instead of ignoring your toddler during a tantrum you could try to comfort them: a tantrum is as scary for them as it is irritating to you and toddlers cannot control their emotions like we can; a big hug is often much more effective and positive in the long term than the usual 'ignore it' advice. Comforting your toddler during and after a tantrum says, 'It's OK, I'm here for you, I love you, and I am strong enough to cope with your big feelings.'

Example 8: The toddler who will not use their potty

Many parents struggle with toilet training, finding the whole process fraught with stress. Lots of toddlers can be difficult to toilet train. Perhaps your toddler will not poo in his potty or perhaps he frequently pees in his bedroom, or perhaps he just has no interest in losing the nappies, even though he is already three and a half? What do you do? Again the CRUCIAL framework can help to steer your actions and help to make toilet training a less stressful experience for all.

Control

Who really has the **control** when it comes to toilet training? The parent or the child? Very often toddlers are not even afforded the control of choosing when the time is right to ditch nappies and begin toilet training, as parents may be concerned about the child's age or the (perceived) need for them to be out of nappies in order to start preschool or nursery. In these instances, though, the toddler has had no say in whether or not they are ready to toilet train, the decision has been made for them and often the lack of control they experience in making this decision is reflected by their unwillingness to cooperate in the process. If potty training is a struggle the chances are that the decision to toilet train was all in your control and your toddler simply isn't ready. This is certainly the key point to consider if you are having trouble with toilet training.

The ultimate control would be allowing your toddler to decide when they are ready to toilet train. If they have decided that now is the right time you can help your toddler to have a little more control, which often results in more cooperation, by giving them choices. You could let them choose their own potty and knickers or pants; or perhaps they could also choose where the potty should be situated, perhaps they would like one in more than one room?

Problems with potty training can also indicate problems with lack of control in other areas of the toddler's life, so think about any wider control you can give them. For example, establish the one-to-one playtime sessions as mentioned in Example 1.

Rhythm

When you are thinking about creating **rhythms** and rituals around toilet training you could sing a toilet-related song that the two of you make up; the funnier and more playful the better. You could let your toddler watch you going to the bathroom so that he knows what to expect and you could read potty-related story books with your toddler, also to provide a sense of expectation and rhythm.

Understanding

Understanding why your child refuses to use the potty is vital. Could it be that it hurts them to do so? They might be constipated; certainly previous constipation issues can lead a toddler to being scared to poo, even once the issues are resolved. The seat itself may be uncomfortable, particularly if their legs are dangling and their feet do not reach the floor or on a stool; aside from feeling a little vulnerable in this position, it always helps if the toddler's feet are on the floor or on a stool as it helps the muscles around their bottom to relax. Your toddler may be scared, particularly in the case of a seat on the big toilet, which may be wobbly and cause them to fear falling in, or perhaps the loud noise of the flush on the big toilet bothers them? They may be embarrassed, if you refer to 'yuck, stinky poo' when you change their nappy, for example. Lastly, consider that, quite often, frequent accidents, or deliberately weeing somewhere, can be a sign of stress in your toddler's life, or then again, perhaps they are just simply not ready to toilet train yet!

Communication

The 'say what you see' approach works well here; many parents may be tempted to use extrinsic rewards such as 'good boy, you did a wee wee' or giving the toddler a sticker or a chocolate for using the potty, but thinking about our knowledge of generic praise we know now that this isn't the best way to help a child to develop internal motivation. Instead you could say, 'I see a little girl sitting on her potty and doing a wee wee!' This kind of **communication** is just enough to show your child that you have noticed their effort and to give her the motivation needed to continue.

Lastly, try never to chastise your toddler for a toilet-related accident. Instead of shouting or punishing them, try saying something like, 'We don't wee on the floor, wee goes in the potty or the nappy,' while calmly clearing up.

Individual

It is impossible to give one answer here as potty training is so unique for each **individual** toddler. Don't be tempted to rush potty training because your nursery or preschool tells you that they would like your toddler out of nappies or hint that they really should be trained by now. Similarly, don't judge your toddler by another. Each child is different, each toddler will be emotionally and physically ready to toilet train at different times. If you wait until your toddler is truly ready you will have a significantly easier time than if you don't!

Avoidance

Does your toddler really need to be potty trained now or could they stay in nappies for a bit longer? I am a firm believer in **avoiding** toilet training for as long as possible. In fact I have never trained any of my four children to use the potty. In each case I waited until they were ready and asked me, either verbally or through their actions, to ditch their nappies and use the toilet. Out of four children I can count the number of potty-related accidents we have had on one hand. I have never found it traumatic, as for each child it was easy, because they led the way. I wish I could take credit for making some sort of well-researched decision, but I can't; at the time I referred to it simply as 'lazy parenting', why would I create all of this work for myself if I didn't need to? Surely if I waited until they did it themselves it would be easier? And it was.

Love

As always, remember it is the toileting behaviour you dislike, not your toddler. They are not having accidents or refusing to use the potty to deliberately annoy you. In fact when a toddler feels safe and secure and unconditionally loved toilet training is often easier. Look back to the advice given in Example 1 for the **Love** aspect of the CRUCIAL framework.

Example 9: The toddler who will not settle at preschool or nursery

For many parents starting preschool is an easy transition and their toddlers happily run in to their new friends each morning with barely a second glance. For others, though, it can be a lot harder, with staff peeling crying toddlers out of your arms and assuring you, 'They will be OK'; you leave wracked with guilt, sad and sometimes angry too, wondering why your toddler can't be like the other children who have no trouble leaving their parents. Is there any way to make this situation easier for everyone involved? The CRUCIAL framework can help to steer your actions and make the transition a less stressful experience for all.

Control

Who really has the **control** when it comes to starting preschool? The parent or the child? Very often toddlers are not even afforded the control of choosing when the time is right for them to leave their parents and start at nursery or preschool; parents may be concerned about the child's age or the (perceived) need for them to receive more stimulation than they do at home, perhaps they feel that preschool or nursery is necessary for their toddler to develop social skills. Sometimes parents need their toddlers to attend nursery so that they may return to work, or spend more time with a new baby. In all of these instances, though, the toddler has had no say in whether or not they are ready to start nursery or preschool, and often the lack of control they experience is reflected by their unwillingness to cooperate in the plans.

If starting nursery is a struggle there is a good chance that the decision to start was all in your control and your toddler simply isn't ready, and this is certainly the key point to consider if you are having trouble with preschool and nursery attendance, although obviously it is not the only cause by any means.

The ultimate control would be allowing your toddler to decide when they are ready to start preschool or nursery. If they have decided that now is the right time you can help your toddler to have a little more control, which often results in more cooperation, by giving them choices. You could let them choose their clothing for nursery, or perhaps a special nursery bag. Or you could entrust them with the control of choosing their preschool or nursery. I think sometimes parents can be too concerned about the reports, reputations and facilities offered in a nursery than checking the most important thing of all, whether their toddler actually likes it there.

A reluctance to attend preschool or nursery is very normal and often just indicative of the fact that your toddler is not yet ready to leave you, but sometimes it can suggest problems with lack of control in other areas of the toddler's life, so think about any wider control you can give them. For example, establish the one-to-one playtime sessions as mentioned in Example 1.

Rhythm

Thinking about creating **rhythms** and rituals around attending nursery or preschool can help to ease the transition. For instance, making a visual calendar, perhaps with photographs you have taken of the nursery building, so that your toddler knows whether or not it is a nursery day, reading books about starting preschool and talking about it the night before can help your toddler know what to expect.

Understanding

Understanding why your child does not want to leave you to go to preschool is vital. Could it be that they are scared you may not come back again? Is there something that scares them at preschool? Is another child particularly noisy or violent towards them? Does something there make a funny noise? Are they encouraged to eat food that they don't like? Or sit in a way that makes them uncomfortable? The reasons are infinite of course.

For many toddlers the fact that they are simply not yet ready to leave you is a common cause of their reluctance. You could choose to listen to this need and keep them at home with you a little longer, but if you need your child to attend nursery because you are returning to work consider ways that you can ease the separation from you, perhaps leaving your toddler with an item that reminds them of you, a comfort or 'transitional' object. You could also suggest to the nursery that you stay with your toddler a bit for the sessions, slowly decreasing the time you stay with them until they are settled without you. Find out who your child's key worker is and try to encourage your child to bond with them as much as possible.

Communication

Remember to 'say what you see': many parents may be tempted to use extrinsic rewards such as saying, 'Good boy, you didn't cry when you went in today' or giving the toddler a sweet for staying at nursery all morning, but this isn't the best way to help a child to develop internal motivation and it does not validate their very real emotions. Instead you could say, 'I see a little boy having fun exploring his new preschool' – this small **communication** is just enough to show your child that you have noticed their effort and to perhaps give him the motivation needed to continue exploring.

Also, think about the theory of modelling here; if you are anxious at leaving your toddler he will surely notice, so perhaps experiment with a few simple relaxation methods so that you remain calm when it is time to leave.

Individual

Don't be tempted to rush your toddler into starting preschool or nursery just because your friend's children all go, or relatives comment, 'Isn't it time he went to nursery by now?' Similarly, don't judge your toddler by another. Each child is an **individual**; each toddler will be emotionally and physically ready to start nursery or preschool at different times. If you can wait until your toddler is truly ready then you will have a significantly easier time than if you don't.

Avoidance

Is it possible to **avoid** the situation? Does your toddler really need to start preschool or nursery now, or could they stay at home for a bit longer? If you need to return to work is there another option that may suit your toddler better, such as staying with a friend or relative that he already knows? Perhaps a childminder or nanny would provide a more homely and less busy environment?

Love

As always remember it is your toddler's behaviour in refusing to go to nursery that you dislike, not your toddler. Far from wanting to upset you their reluctance to leave you actually shows how much your toddler loves you. Look back to the advice given in Example 1 for the **Love** aspect of the CRUCIAL framework.

Example 10: The toddler with a new sibling

For many parents of toddlers a new baby in the family can be not only a time of joy, but also a time of immense stress. Understandably some toddlers do not take too well to the transition to being an older sibling. Some parents are concerned about any effects on their toddler and seek to minimise the disruption in advance. I am commonly asked for tips to help toddlers to adjust to life with a new baby in the family, and yet again the CRUCIAL framework can help to make the introduction of a new member of the family a less stressful experience for all.

Control

There are two big points to consider here, the first being the obvious fact that your toddler has had no **control** over when they became an older brother or sister, and while we obviously consider the needs of our toddler when deciding to have another baby we very rarely ask their opinion.

The second major point is that when we have another baby suddenly our toddlers seem huge to us in comparison to our tiny newborns. Very often we expect them to behave in a more mature way too, often forgetting that, really, they are still babies too. This can often leave toddlers with what we call in ToddlerCalm™ classes, 'The wanting to be big versus the wanting to be small complex.' Most toddlers want 'to be grown up', they want the freedom and the control that 'being big' brings, however, this can often be at odds with their primal need to be nurtured, or to 'be small'.

When there is a new tiny baby in the family we can often unwittingly force our toddlers to 'be big', commonly saying things like, 'You're a big boy now' or 'You're not a baby any more.' Toddlers are often moved from parents' beds or rooms or from their cot or nursery into 'a big boy bedroom' or 'a big girl bed'. This can leave them in a horrible position of having unmet needs and feelings that are not validated, which are only exacerbated by the arrival of a new baby. In many ways expecting your toddler 'to be big' when a new baby arrives is almost forcing more control on them than they are ready for, while taking away the control of their security of your constant availability to them.

Rather than deciding when your toddler is ready to move into a new room or a new bed consider giving them some control by allowing your toddler to decide when they are ready to move from your bed, your room or their cot or nursery. Similarly giving them the control of deciding when they are ready to give up their baby toys and the bottle or breast can really help them to adjust to the new baby.

If your toddler is your firstborn, think about the fact that for their entire life they have had your undivided attention and availability, both emotional and physical. When the new baby arrives your attention and availability are dramatically diminished. Naturally this can be unsettling to many toddlers and it is important for them to realise that you are still there when they need you, as well as having time to be just the two of you again, with nobody else to share your attention. For example, establish the one-to-one playtime sessions as mentioned in Example 1.

Lastly also think about giving your toddler more control in his role as a big brother by giving him special jobs to help with the baby, perhaps he could fetch a clean nappy for you or entertain the baby while you change a nappy. Perhaps he could sing a lullaby each night or help to dry the baby after a bath. By helping your toddler to feel important to the new baby you will help him to feel more in control too.

Rhythm

Perhaps the best thing you can do to maintain a sense of **rhythm** here is trying to help your toddler to understand what is about to happen. Sharing books about new baby siblings, talking about pregnancy and birth and what will happen once the baby arrives is really important. Explain to your toddler that babies need to feed a lot and that they will cry and wake up a lot at night too, and also explain that we must be gentle with them and keep toys and food away from them too. As well as sharing books there are some great video clips of new babies and gentle births that can be found online.

Remember that your toddler is reassured by predictability, so, while responding to his cues, try to keep his life as constant as possible once your new baby arrives, and that means sticking to his bedtime routine as much as possible and any other rituals you have, including attending nursery and preschool, but be mindful that he may want to be with you for a while until he is used to the new arrival.

Understanding

Understanding means helping your toddler to understand what is about to happen and indeed what is happening once the baby arrives can really help when a new baby is born. Also try to understand your toddler's reactions too. I have heard many parents complain that their toddler 'has been a terror since the baby was born', but I am always surprised at how few have really explored the effect a new baby may have had on their toddler and the emotions that have resulted. Showing your toddler empathy here really is the key.

Communication

A very useful way of **communicating** what life will be like with a new baby and indeed translating the behaviour you expect from your toddler once the baby has arrived into a language that toddlers will understand is role play. Getting a baby doll for your toddler and perhaps a sling or carrier and a tiny nappy and some clothes can help to foster empathy and gentle behaviour in your toddler towards 'their baby'. This very often then will translate into similar behaviour with their 'real life' baby. Toddlers love to model our behaviour and if we are feeding or soothing their baby sibling you could encourage them to look after 'their baby' too.

Using the 'say what you see' approach again works well here rather than using extrinsic rewards for good behaviour: for instance, you could say, 'I see a little girl who is being very kind to the baby' or 'I see a little boy who is very sad that mummy can't play because the baby is feeding again, I wish I could play too.' Try never to chastise your toddler for an incident involving the new baby. Instead of shouting or punishing your toddler if they wake the baby, try saying something like, 'We don't shout at the baby, we talk with gentle voices when he sleeps.' Remember the importance of validating your toddler's feelings; understand that brushing their concerns or fears aside does not make them go away. Instead of saying, 'Don't be silly, of course

I still love you, that's a silly thing to say' try to acknowledge their emotions and respond, 'I think you are worried that I don't love you now the baby is here, but I do, I have more than enough love for both of you.'

Individual

Each child is an **individual**, each toddler will respond emotionally and physically differently at the arrival of a new sibling. Some will take to it with ease, quickly forming a bond, helping and generally being a joy to have around, whereas others may really struggle. There is no right or wrong way for a toddler to respond to the birth of a new sibling, only their way, and frustratingly 'their way' is almost impossible to predict.

Avoidance

Of course you cannot **avoid** your new baby, but are there ways that you can avoid the baby having such a large impact on your toddler? For instance, investing in a good sling or carrier and learning to 'babywear' can be a godsend to a parent with a toddler or a newborn. Newborns don't really need much more than warmth, food, nappy changes and physical contact with you in the early days and are usually very happy to spend most of their day attached to your chest in a carrier. This then leaves you with two free hands to entertain your toddler, so both children will have their needs met. I cannot recommend this enough. A well-selected carrier or sling will allow you to enjoy almost everything you did with your toddler before the birth of the baby.

Love

As always remember it is the behaviour of your toddler around the baby that you dislike, not your toddler. Spending one-to-one 'special time' with each individual child that you have is vital, particularly as they grow. The special time may change as they get older; it may not involve play any more, instead it may involve just hugging, talking or just 'being there' if the child wants you, but the need for one-to-one contact and connection never disappears.

This idea has been expanded upon by English psychologist Oliver James in his book *Love Bombing*. James describes the technique, saying, 'Love Bombing gives your child a very intense, condensed experience of feeling completely loved and completely in control,' also picking up on the idea that very often it is not just the child who needs to reconnect, saying 'most of us need to reconnect with our children from time to time. Love Bombing does the job.' Oliver also agrees with giving your child a memento or reminder of you, in particular relating to a special time you have spent together, commenting, 'The object becomes a safe haven in stormy weather ... you can get the memento out and talk about the special time using it as a prop to remind him of that calmer, better time together.'

Look back to the advice given in Example 1 for the **Love** aspect of the CRUCIAL framework. I cannot stress how important this advice is here; it is absolutely critical that you take care of your own needs while trying to balance those of your toddler and your newborn.

Close

I hope these worked examples have given you a good grasp of how to apply the CRUCIAL framework to your own issues with your own toddler. Combining this approach with new knowledge of your toddler's brain development and new expectations of their sleep and eating will hopefully help you to understand your toddler and his actions a little better.

I hope that it will now be easier for you to distinguish your feelings from your toddler and your toddler's behaviour and to realise that far from being a manipulative little tyrant your toddler is in fact an amazing, entertaining little companion full of love and wonder. When we understand our toddlers a little more and stop viewing the toddler years as a battle that needs to be won, we inevitably find that toddlers can be such fun to be around and far from being something to wish away as quickly as possible, the toddler years really can be terrific, and they certainly do go too quickly.

In your quest to understand and calm your toddler please take time to remember how important you are though. You are important, not just for your communication and modelling of the behaviour you want to see in your toddler, but also for your own sake as an individual, which highlights the importance of nurturing yourself and finding another container to offload your parental stresses to. I do believe the key to calmer toddlers really does lie in the hands of the parents, and in something that can be a wonderful, ever-perpetuating cycle of calmness and happiness, calmer toddlers really do make for happier parents, just as happier parents make for calmer toddlers. I hope my book has given you all that you need to turn this into a reality.

Good luck!

Resources

Resources for parents of toddlers in the UK

TodderCalm™ – UK-wide classes for parents of toddlers
www.toddlercalm.co.uk

ToddlerCalm™ on Facebook
www.facebook.com/toddlercalm

ToddlerCalm™ on Twitter
www.twitter.com/toddlercalm

Sarah Ockwell-Smith's personal blog
www.sarahockwell-smith.com

Attachment Parenting UK
www.attachmentparenting.co.uk

ISIS – Infant Sleep Information Source
www.isisonline.org.uk

Centre for Non-Violent Communication
www.cnvc.org

Relax Kids – UK-wide kids relaxation classes and CD
www.relaxkids.com

Birthlight – UK-wide toddler swimming and yoga classes
www.birthlight.com

Family Lives – free telephone helpline for parents
www.familylives.org.uk

Gingerbread – supporting single parents
www.gingerbread.org.uk

Homestart – family support charity
www.home-start.org.uk

PANDAS – support for prenatal and postnatal depression
www.pandasfoundation.org.uk

Stonewall – supporting same-sex parents
www.stonewall.org.uk

Montessori UK – Montessori education in the UK
www.montessori.org.uk

Steiner Waldorf – Steiner education in the UK
www.steinerwaldorf.org.uk

Forest Education Initiative – outdoor learning
www.foresteducation.org

Bestbear – listing of tested and vetted nanny agencies
www.bestbear.co.uk

ERIC – help for enuresis (bed wetting)
www.eric.org.uk

ICAN – helping children to communicate
www.ican.org.uk

Talking Point – children's communication information
www.talkingpoint.org.uk

Sling Meet – help with choosing a toddler carrier
www.slingmeet.co.uk

Little Signer's Club – toddler sign language classes
www.littlesignersclub.co.uk

Oliver James Love Bombing
www.lovebombing.info

Woodcraft Folk – Woodchips toddler group
www.woodcraft.org.uk/woodchips

The LaLeche League UK – breastfeeding help and advice
www.laleche.org.uk

The Breastfeeding Network – breastfeeding help and advice
www.breastfeedingnetwork.org.uk

Association of Breastfeeding Mothers – breastfeeding help
www.abm.me.uk

Resources for parents of toddlers in Ireland

TodderCalm™ – workshops and classes for parents of toddlers
www.toddlercalming.com

ToddlerCalm™ on Facebook
www.facebook.com/toddlercalm

ToddlerCalm™ on Twitter
www.twitter.com/toddlercalm

Sarah Ockwell-Smith's personal blog
www.sarahockwell-smith.com

Attachment Parenting International
www.attachmentparenting.com

ISIS – Infant Sleep Information Source
www.isisonline.org.uk

Centre for Non-Violent Communication
www.cnvc.org

Relax Kids – relaxation CDs and resources
www.relaxkids.com

Birthlight – toddler swimming and yoga classes
www.birthlight.com

Gingerbread – supporting single parents
www.gingerbread.ie

Homestart – family support charity
www.homestartireland.ie

Montessori – Montessori education in Ireland
www.montessoriireland.ie

Steiner Waldorf – Steiner education in Ireland
www.steinerireland.org

ICAN – helping children to communicate
www.ican.org.uk

Talking Point – children's communication information
www.talkingpoint.org.uk

Babywearing Ireland – help with choosing a toddler carrier
www.babywearingireland.ie

Oliver James Love Bombing
www.lovebombing.info

The LaLeche League – breastfeeding help and advice
www.lalecheleagueireland.com

Resources for parents of toddlers in Australia

TodderCalm™ – workshops and classes for parents of toddlers
www.toddlercalming.com

ToddlerCalm™ on Facebook
www.facebook.com/toddlercalm

ToddlerCalm™ on Twitter
www.twitter.com/toddlercalm

Sarah Ockwell-Smith's personal blog
www.sarahockwell-smith.com

Attachment Parenting Australia
www.attachmentparentingaustralia.com

ISIS – Infant Sleep Information Source
www.isisonline.org.uk

Centre for Non-Violent Communication
www.cnvc.org

Relax Kids – relaxation CDs and resources
www.relaxkids.com

Birthlight – toddler swimming and yoga classes
www.birthlight.com

Montessori – Montessori education in Australia
www.montessori.org.au

Steiner Waldorf – Steiner education in Australia
www.steiner-australia.org

Nurture Magazine
www.nurtureparentingmagazine.com.au

Oliver James Love Bombing
www.lovebombing.info

The LaLeche League – breastfeeding help and advice
www.lalecheleague.org.nz

Resources for parents of toddlers in Canada

TodderCalm™ – workshops and classes for parents of toddlers
www.toddlercalming.com

ToddlerCalm™ on Facebook
www.facebook.com/toddlercalm

ToddlerCalm™ on Twitter
www.twitter.com/toddlercalm

Sarah Ockwell-Smith's personal blog
www.sarahockwell-smith.com

Attachment Parenting Canada
www.attachmentparenting.ca

ISIS – Infant Sleep Information Source
www.isisonline.org.uk

Centre for Non-Violent Communication
www.cnvc.org

Relax Kids – relaxation CDs and resources
www.relaxkids.com

Montessori – Montessori education Canada
www.montessorisocietycanada.org/

Steiner Waldorf – Steiner education in Canada
www.waldorf.ca

Oliver James Love Bombing
www.lovebombing.info

The LaLeche League – breastfeeding help and advice
www.lllc.ca

Resources for parents of toddlers in New Zealand

TodderCalm™ – workshops and classes for parents of toddlers
www.toddlercalming.com

ToddlerCalm™ on Facebook
www.facebook.com/toddlercalm

ToddlerCalm™ on Twitter
www.twitter.com/toddlercalm

Sarah Ockwell-Smith's personal blog
www.sarahockwell-smith.com

The Natural Parent – NZ natural parenting magazine
www.thenaturalparent.co.nz

ISIS – Infant Sleep Information Source
www.isisonline.org.uk

Playcentre – supporting parents and toddlers through play
www.playcentre.org.nz

Centre for Non-Violent Communication
www.cnvc.org

Peaceful Parent Institute – gentle parenting support
www.peaceful-parent.com

Parent 2 Parent – supporting parents of toddlers with
disabilities
www.parent2parent.org.nz

Toy Library Federation of New Zealand
www.toylibrary.co.nz

Relax Kids – relaxation CDs and resources
www.relaxkids.com

Birthlight – toddler swimming and yoga classes
www.birthlight.com

Montessori – Montessori education in New Zealand
www.montessori.org.nz

Steiner Waldorf – Steiner education in New Zealand
www.rudolfsteinerfederation.org.nz

Oliver James Love Bombing
www.lovebombing.info

The LaLeche League – breastfeeding help and advice
www.lalecheleague.org.nz

Resources for parents of toddlers in South Africa

TodderCalm™ – workshops and classes for parents of toddlers
www.toddlercalming.com

ToddlerCalm™ on Facebook
www.facebook.com/toddlercalm

ToddlerCalm™ on Twitter
www.twitter.com/toddlercalm

Sarah Ockwell-Smith's personal blog
www.sarahockwell-smith.com

Attachment Parenting International
www.attachmentparenting.com

ISIS – Infant Sleep Information Source
www.isisonline.org.uk

Centre for Non-Violent Communication
www.cnvc.org

Relax Kids – relaxation CDs and resources
www.relaxkids.com

Birthlight – toddler swimming and yoga classes
www.birthlight.com

Montessori – Montessori education in South Africa
www.samontessori.org.za

Steiner Waldorf – Steiner education in South Africa
www.waldorf.org.za

Oliver James Love Bombing
www.lovebombing.info

The LaLeche League – breastfeeding help and advice
www.llli.org/southafrica.html

Resources for parents of toddlers in the USA

TodderCalm™ – workshops and classes for parents of toddlers
www.toddlercalming.com

ToddlerCalm™ on Facebook
www.facebook.com/toddlercalm

ToddlerCalm™ on Twitter
www.twitter.com/toddlercalm

Sarah Ockwell-Smith's personal blog
www.sarahockwell-smith.com

Attachment Parenting International
www.attachmentparenting.com

ISIS – Infant Sleep Information Source
www.isisonline.org.uk

Centre for Non-Violent Communication
www.cnvc.org

Relax Kids – relaxation CDs and resources
www.relaxkids.com

Birthlight – toddler swimming and yoga classes
www.birthlight.com

Montessori – Montessori education
www.montessori.org

Oliver James Love Bombing
www.lovebombing.info

The LaLeche League – breastfeeding help and advice
www.llli.org/webus.html

Recommended products

All available worldwide from www.toddlercalming.com

ToddlerCalm™ Toddler Relaxation Sleep CD: for part of your three step bedtime routine

Aromafan battery operated aromatherapy fan diffuser: for part of your three step bedtime routine

Lavender or Roman chamomile essential oil: for part of your three step bedtime routine

Toddler massage oil: for part of your three step bedtime routine

Cuski comforter: a great 'transitional object'

Mini Moby doll sling: perfect for role playing for new big brothers and sisters

The Tula toddler carrier: a great toddler carrier

Bibliography

J. Bowlby, *A Secure Base*, Routledge (2005).

L. Cohen, *Playful Parenting*, Ballantine Books (2012).

L. Davis, *Becoming the Parent You Want to Be*, Bantam Doubleday Dell (2000).

S. Gerhardt, *Why Love Matters: How Affection Shapes a Baby's Brain*, Routledge (2004).

J. Holt, *How Children Learn*, Penguin (1991).

D. Jackson, *Three in a Bed*, Bloomsbury (2003).

O. James, *Love Bombing*, Karnac Books (2012).

A. Kohn, *Punished by Rewards: The Trouble with Gold Stars, Incentive Plans, A's, Praise and Other Bribes*, Houghton Mifflin (2000).

H. Lee, *To Kill a Mockingbird: 50th Anniversary Edition*, Arrow (2010).

P. D. MacLean, *The Triune Brain in Evolution: Role in Paleocerebral Functions*, Springer (1990).

A. Miller, *For Your Own Good: The Roots of Violence in Child-Rearing*, Virago (1987).

J. Nelsen, *Positive Discipline: The First Three Years: From Infant to Toddler – Laying the Foundation for Raising a Capable, Confident Child*, Three Rivers Press (2007).

G. Rapley, *Baby-led Weaning: Helping your Baby to Love Good Food*, Vermilion (2008).

D. Siegel and T. Payne Bryson, *The Whole-Brain Child: 12 Proven Strategies to Nurture Your Child's Developing Mind*, Robinson (2012).

M. Sunderland, *What Every Parent Needs to Know*, Dorling Kindersley (2007).

K. Uvnes-Moburg, *The Oxytocin Factor: Tapping the Hormone of Calm, Love and Healing*, Pinter and Martin (2011).

D. Winnicott, *The Family and Individual Development*, Routledge (2006).

References

1. M.A. Barnett, 'Empathy and related responses in children'. In: N. Eisenberg and J. Strayer (eds), *Empathy and its Development,* New York: Cambridge University Press (1987).

2. R. Kestenbaum, E.A. Farber and L.A. Sroufe, 'Individual differences in empathy among preschoolers: relation to attachment history'. In: N. Eisenberg and J. Strayer (eds), *Empathy and its Development,* New York: Cambridge University Press (1987).

3. H. Rao, L. Betancourt, J.M. Giannetta, N.L. Brodsky, M. Korczykowski, B.B. Avants, J.C. Gee, J. Wang, H. Hurt, J.A. Detre and M.J. Farah, 'Early parental care is important for hippocampal maturation: evidence from brain morphology in humans', *Neuroimage* (2010).

4. M. Weinraub, R.H.I. Bender, S. Friedman, E.J. Susman, B. Knoke, R. Bradley *et al.*, 'Patterns of developmental change in infants' nighttime sleep awakenings from 6 to 36 months of age', *Child Development* (2012); 48: 1511–28.

5. T.F. Anders, L.F. Halpern and J. Hua, 'Sleeping through the night: a developmental perspective', *Pediatrics* (1992); 90:554–60.

6. K.L. Armstrong, R.A. Quinn and M.R. Dadds, 'The sleep patterns of normal children', *Medical Journal of Australia* (1994) 1 Aug; 161(3):202–6.

7. C. Kirschbaum, R. Steyer, M. Eid, U. Patalla, P. Schwenkmezger and D. Hellhammer, 'Cortisol and behaviour', *Psychoneuroendrocrinology* (1990); 15:297–307.

8. C. Torres-Farfan, V. Rocco, C. Monsó, F.J. Valenzuela, G. Campino, A. Germain, F. Torrealba, G.J. Valenzuela and M. Seron-Ferre,

'Maternal melatonin effects on clock gene expression in a nonhuman primate fetus', *Endocrinology* (2006); 147(10):4618–26.

9. M. Silva, M. Mallozi and G. Ferrari, 'Salivary cortisol to assess the hypothalamic-pituitary-adrenal axis in healthy children under 3 years old', *Jornal De Pediatria* (2007); 83(2):121–26.

10. S. Watamura, E. Kryzer and S. Robertson, 'Cortisol patterns at home and child care: afternoon differences and evening recovery in children attending very high quality full-day center-based child care', *Journal of Applied Developmental Psychology* (2009); 30:475–85.

11. A.C. Dettling, M.R. Gunnar and B. Donzella, 'Cortisol levels of young children in full-day childcare centers: relations with age and temperament', *Psychoneuroendocrinology* (1999); 24:519–36.

12. A.C. Dettling, S.W. Parker, S. Lane, A. Sebanc and M.R. Gunnar, 'Quality of care and temperament determine changes in cortisol concentrations over the day for young children in childcare', *Psychoneuroendocrinology* (2000); 25:819–36.

13. K.L. Armstrong, R.A. Quinn and M.R. Dadds, 'The sleep patterns of normal children', *Medical Journal of Australia* (1994) 1 Aug; 161(3):202–6.

14. W. Middlemiss, D.A. Granger, W.A. Goldberg and L. Nathans, 'Asynchrony of mother-infant hypothalamic-pituitary-adrenal axis activity following extinction of infant crying responses induced during the transition to sleep', *Early Human Development* (2012); 88(4): 227–32.

15. M. Weinraub, R.H.I. Bender, S. Friedman, E.J. Susman, B. Knoke, R. Bradley *et al.*, 'Patterns of developmental change in infants' nighttime sleep awakenings from 6 to 36 months of age', *Child Development* (2012); 48: 1511–28.

16. A.M. Price, M. Wake *et al.*, 'Five-year follow-up of harms and benefits of behavioral infant sleep intervention: randomized trial', *Pediatrics*. Published online 10 September 2012.

17. J.A. Mindell, L.S. Telofski, B. Wiegand and E.S. Kurtz, 'A nightly bedtime routine: impact on sleep in young children and maternal mood', *Sleep* (2009) May; 32(5):599–606.

18. C.M. Wright, K.N. Parkinson, D. Shipton and R.F. Drewett, 'How do toddler eating problems relate to their eating behavior, food preferences, and growth?' *Pediatrics* (2007) Oct; 120(4):1069–75.

19. K. Cowbrough, 'Feeding the toddler: 12 months to 3 years – challenges and opportunities', *Journal of Family Health Care* (2010); 20(2):49–52.

20. L.L. Birch, 'Development of food acceptance patterns in the first years of life', *Proceedings of the Nutriton Society* (1998) Nov; 57(4):617–24.

21. E. Townsend and N.J. Pitchford, 'Baby knows best? The impact of weaning style on food preferences and body mass index in early childhood in a case-controlled sample' (2012), in print.

22. D. Benton, 'Role of parents in the determination of the food preferences of children and the development of obesity', *International Journal of Obesity and Related Metabolic Disorders* (2004) Jul; 28(7):858–69.

23. J.A. Mennella, M. Yanina Pepino and D.R. Reed, 'Genetic and environmental determinants of bitter perception and sweet preferences', *Pediatrics* (2005); 115(2):e216–e222.

24. F. Warneken and M. Tomasello, 'Extrinsic rewards undermine altruistic tendencies in 20-month-olds', *Developmental Psychology* (2008) Nov; 44(6):1785–8.

25. R.A. Fabes, J. Fulse, N. Eisenberg *et al.*, 'Effects of rewards on children's prosocial motivation: a socialization study', *Developmental Psychology* (1989); 25:509–15.

26. N. Eisenberg, R.A. Fabes and T.L. Spinrad, 'Prosocial development'. In: W. Damon (ed.), *Handbook of Child Psychology, volume 3: Social, emotional, and personality development*, 5th edition, New York: Wiley (2006).

27. J. Henderlong and M.R. Lepper, 'The effects of praise on children's intrinsic motivation: a review and synthesis', *Psychological Bulletin* (2002); 128(5):774–95.

28. E. Meins, C. Fernyhough, B. Arnott, S. Leekam and M. Turner, 'Mother- versus infant-centred correlates of maternal mind-mindedness in the first year of life', *Infancy* (2011); 16:137–65.

29. B. Arnott and E. Meins, 'Continuity in mind-mindedness from pregnancy to the first year of life', *Infant Behavior and Development*, (2008); 31:647–54.

30. G. Domes, M. Heinrichs, A. Michel, C. Berger and S.C. Herpertz, 'Oxytocin improves "mind-reading" in humans', *Biological Psychiatry* (2007) 15 March; 61(6):731–3.

Index

Note: page numbers in *italics* refer to information contained within tables and diagrams.